THE IMMORTAL IRON FIST

THE BOOK OF THE IRON FIST

THE
IMMORTAL
IRON
FIST

THE BOOK OF THE IRON FIST

Writers: Matt Fraction
with Ed Brubaker (Issue #7)

ISSUE #7
Artists: Travel Foreman & Derek Fridolfs, Leandro Fernandez
& Francisco Paronzini and Khari Evans & Victor Olazaba
Colorist: Dan Brown • Cover Art: Travel Foreman & Len O'Grady

ISSUE #15
Artists: Khari Evans & Victor Olazaba
Colorists: Jelena Kevic Djurdjevic & Paul Mounts
Cover Art: Khari Evans, Victor Olazaba & Matt Hollingsworth

ORSON RANDALL & THE GREEN MIST OF DEATH
Artists: Nick Dragotta, Mike Allred, Russ Heath, Lewis LaRosa &
Stefano Gaudiano and Mitch Breitweiser
Colorists: Laura Allred, Russ Heath & Matt Hollingsworth
Cover Art: Kaare Andrews

ISSUE #16
Artist: David Aja • Colorist: Matt Hollingsworth • Cover Art: David Aja
Letterers: Dave Lanphear & Artmonkeys Studios
Assistant Editor: Alejandro Arbona • Editor: Warren Simons

THE ORIGIN OF DANNY RAND
Writers: Roy Thomas, Len Wein & Matt Fraction
Pencilers: Gil Kane, Larry Hama & Kano
Inkers: Dick Giordano & Kano
Colorists: Sotocolor's A. Crossley & Kano
Letterer: L.P. Gregory & Dave Lanphear
Cover Artists: Gil Kane, Larry Hama & Rain Beredo

Collection Editor: Jennifer Grünwald • Editorial Assistant: Alex Starbuck
Assistant Editors: Cory Levine & John Denning
Editor, Special Projects: Mark D. Beazley
Senior Editor, Special Projects: Jeff Youngquist
Senior Vice President of Sales: David Gabriel • Production: Rodolfo Muraguchi
Vice President of Creative: Tom Marvelli

Editor in Chief: Joe Quesada • Publisher: Dan Buckley

IMMORTAL IRON FIST VOL. 3: THE BOOK OF THE IRON FIST. Contains material originally published in magazine form as IMMORTAL IRON FIST #7 and #15-16, IMMORTAL IRON FIST: ORSON RANDALL AND THE GREEN MIST OF DEATH and IMMORTAL IRON FIST: THE ORIGIN OF DANNY RAND. First printing 2008. Hardcover ISBN# 978-0-7851-2993-6. Softcover ISBN# 978-0-7851-2536-5. Published by MARVEL PUBLISHING, INC., a subsidiary of MARVEL ENTERTAINMENT, INC. OFFICE OF PUBLICATION: 417 5th Avenue, New York, NY 10016. Copyright © 2007 and 2008 Marvel Characters, Inc. All rights reserved. Hardcover: $24.99 per copy in the U.S. and $26.50 in Canada (GST #R127032852). Softcover: $16.99 per copy in the U.S. and $17.99 in Canada (GST #R127032852). Canadian Agreement #40668537. All characters featured in this issue and the distinctive names and likenesses thereof, and all related indicia are trademarks of Marvel Characters, Inc. No similarity between any of the names, characters, persons, and/or institutions in this magazine with those of any living or dead person or institution is intended, and any such similarity which may exist is purely coincidental. **Printed in the U.S.A.** ALAN FINE, CEO Marvel Toys & Publishing Divisions and CMO Marvel Characters, Inc.; DAVID GABRIEL, SVP of Publishing Sales & Circulation; DAVID BOGART, SVP of Business Affairs & Talent Management; MICHAEL PASCIULLO, VP of Merchandising & Communications; JIM O'KEEFE, VP of Operations & Logistics; DAN CARR, Executive Director of Publishing Technology; JUSTIN F. GABRIE, Director of Editorial Operations; SUSAN CRESPI, Editorial Operations Manager; OMAR OTIEKU, Production Manager; STAN LEE, Chairman Emeritus. For information regarding advertising in Marvel Comics or on Marvel.com, please contact Mitch Dane, Advertising Director, at mdane@marvel.com. For Marvel subscription inquiries, please call 800-217-9158.

10 9 8 7 6 5 4 3 2 1

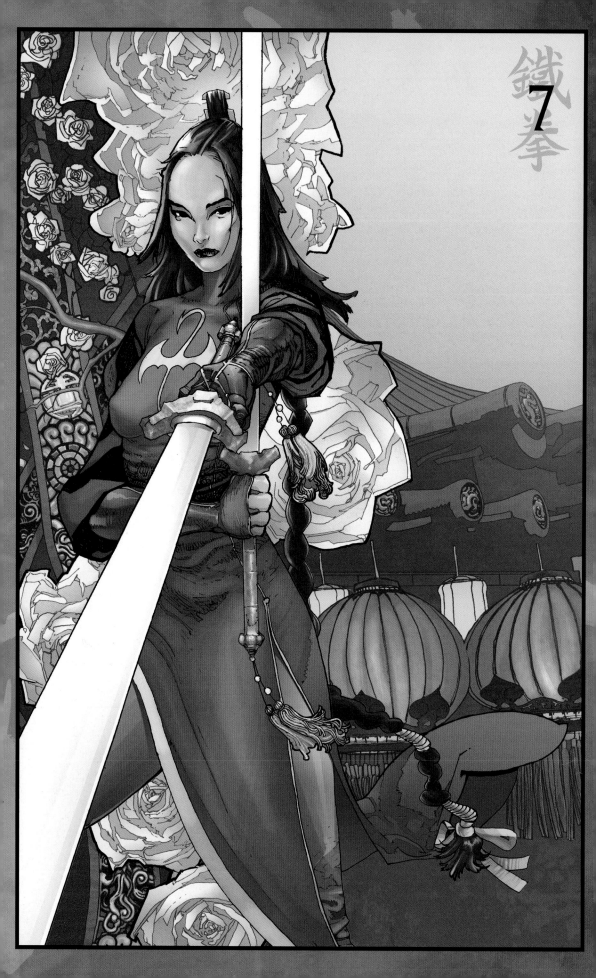

There have been sixty-six men and women to carry the mantle of THE
IMMORTAL IRON FIST throughout the ages, men and women of great
courage, valor, skill, and sacrifice. Sixty-six men and women have
stood between man and the unstoppable forces of evil, willing to give
all they have to hold back the hordes.

This is the story of one of them, as told in THE BOOK OF THE IRON FIST.

The Story of the Iron Fist Wu Ao-Shi

The Pirate Queen of Pinghai Bay

ED BRUBAKER & MATT FRACTION – WRITERS
TRAVEL FOREMAN – ARTIST 1-6
DEREK FRIDOLFS – INKER 1-6
LEANDRO FERNANDEZ – ARTIST 7-13
FRANCISCO PARONZINI AND LEO FERNANDEZ
– INKERS 7-13
KHARI EVANS – ARTIST 14-22
VICTOR OLAZABA – INKER 14-22
DAN BROWN – COLORIST
DAVE LANPHEAR LETTERER
BRAD JOHANSEN - PRODUCTION
ALEJANDRO ARBONA – ASSISTANT EDITOR
WARREN SIMONS – EDITOR
JOE QUESADA – EDITOR IN CHIEF
DAN BUCKLEY – PUBLISHER

Even as a young girl, Wu Ao-Shi was thought of as a difficult woman.

SCAPEGRACE! SCOFFLAW!

I ASK OF YOU-- IS *THIS* THE FACE OF A DUTIFUL CITIZEN OF K'UN-LUN?

I AM BUT A MODEST VENDOR OF GLASS *ROSE-BLOSSOM CHERRIES*--

--THE FINEST IN ALL K'UN-LUN--

AND THIS *SNEAK THIEF* SHAMES MY HARD WORK AND OUR *SACRED CITY* WITH HER *LOW BEHAVIOR.*

WHERE SHALL WE FIND *JUSTICE* FOR THE WORKING MAN?

WHERE SHALL HE FIND HIS HARD-EARNED *RECOMPENSE?*

I SAY, LET IT *COME* FROM THE WORKING MAN! LET IT COME FROM THE *STREETS!*

KKFF-WWHACK

She never let it get her *down.*

Now, maybe **Lei Kung the Thunderer** had a soft spot in his warrior's heart for **difficult women**, or maybe he just saw the spark of greatness in Wu-Ao Shi's eyes...

NOW. *AGAIN.*

A BROKEN BLOSSOM FOR A BROKEN BLOSSOM. TWO FOR EACH OF THE SIX YOU TRIED TO STEAL.

WHAT DO YOU HAVE TO SAY ABOUT *THAT?* NOT SO CUNNING *NOW*, ARE YOU?

KKFTCH

DURR---

YOU. *GIRL.*

STAY *QUIET,* LITTLE ONE. EVEN IF YOU'VE NEVER MANAGED TO STAY QUIET *ONCE* IN YOUR MISERABLE LIFE, I IMPLORE YOU TO *STAY QUIET* NOW.

NOT ONLY SHOULD IT HEAL *UNDISTURBED* BUT, LOOKING AT YOU, I GET THE FEELING...

...THAT WHEN YOU *DO* OPEN YOUR MOUTH, ALL KINDS OF *HELL* FOLLOW.

IF YOU LISTEN TO ME, I WILL SAVE YOUR LIFE.

YOU ARE WELCOME TO CHALLENGE THE ASSERTION.

EXCELLENT.

I AM LEI KUNG THE THUNDERER AND I SAW EVERYTHING.

THIS GIRL DEFENDED HERSELF AGAINST A WELL-KNOWN *NEIGHBORHOOD SCOUNDREL...*

This was the day that Wu Ao-Shi was set upon the path of the Immortal Iron Fist.

And in spite of the many beatings she took over the many years after that day, Wu Ao-Shi never once regretted it...

HOW IS THIS *FAIR*? A *BIG MAN* LIKE YOU, BEATING ON A *LITTLE GIRL* LIKE ME.

LITTLE GIRL. LITTLE. GIRL. UNDERSTAND THIS, *LITTLE GIRL*, FOR WHAT FOLLOWS IS A LESSON I WISH TO TEACH BUT...

...ONCE!

FWHAM

NOTHING WILL BE GIVEN TO YOU IN THIS LIFE!

EVERY COMFORT AND PRIVILEGE YOU MAY KNOW...

...YOU WILL HAVE TO *EARN*.

OR FIGHT FOR.

OR TAKE.

AND THAT IS *NOT* FAIR.

THAT, MY PUPIL, IS *LIFE*, AND IT DOES NOT CARE IF YOU THRIVE OR *STARVE*.

NOW *REPEAT* IT.

LIFE DOES NOT CARE IF I THRIVE...

"...OR STARVE."

EXCUSE ME.

YOU WANT A FISH?

YOU LOOK HUNGRY.

...WHAT?

WHY WOULD YOU JUST *GIVE* ME A FISH?

BECAUSE YOU'RE SITTING HERE ALONE, EATING PLAIN RICE, AND YOU *STILL* LOOK HUNGRY.

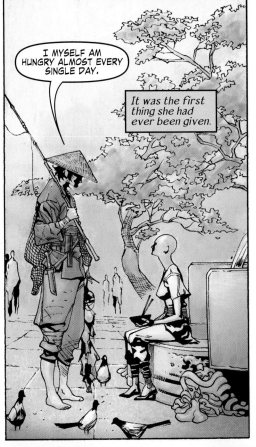

I MYSELF AM HUNGRY ALMOST EVERY SINGLE DAY.

It was the first thing she had ever been given.

And a fine start to their lives together.

I DON'T REMEMBER THE LAST TIME A MAN *TOUCHED ME* AND WASN'T *PUNCHING* ME.

They were in **love**.

It was cute.

Not cloying, but cute. They were a nice couple.

Then one day, the fisherman made a discovery that, even in the middle of a tale such as this, bears repeating with a sense of awe and wonder:

Two **perfect rings** made of the purest silver.

Now, **who** those rings belonged to and **how** they got **inside a fish** is a tale for another time, but in the here and now, our young fisherman knew what to do:

I LOVE YOU BECAUSE WHILE YOU WERE WADING THROUGH FISH GUTS, YOU WERE THINKING OF ME.

OF *COURSE* I WILL BE YOUR BRIDE.

But Wu Ao-Shi was set on the path of the Iron Fist, K'un-Lun's Immortal Weapon. A warrior infused with the life force of a mighty dragon's heart. But to become Iron Fist...

...THE *PERILS* INVOLVED FAR OUTWEIGH THE *REWARD!*

ARE YOU READY TO RISK *DEATH* TO GAIN THE POWER OF *THE IRON FIST?!*

...you must *take* that life force.

YES, I AM READY.

Many that came before Wu Ao-Shi have thought that they were ready, too.

But they weren't. Just as she wasn't.

Neither was he.

And that, dear reader, was the contradiction at the heart of these two:

She was a **weapon** waiting to be wielded upon the wicked in the name of the heavenly city of K'un-Lun.

He caught fish.

HO, ARCHAIC ONE! I COME TO *TAKE* THAT WHICH ONLY I MAY OWN!

How could he live knowing his love was destined to be the first woman who dared face the ancient menace of...

...Shou-Lao, the Undying!

The ancient and venerated beast that protects K'un-Lun in between the eras of its Immortal Weapon.

Many of K'un-Lun's finest citizenry were there at Wu Ao-Shi's challenge.

Some of them wanted to witness the next Iron Fist's **birth**. Others wished to witness Wu Ao-Shi's **death**.

But all of them-- save **one**--actually **watched**.

K'un-Lun is a place without many clocks...

And with few people interested in watching them...

But if it wasn't...

And if they were...

They'd have seen that none before her had felled the beast as quickly as she.

She was Wu Ao-Shi when she walked into the cave...

...And **the Immortal Iron Fist** when she strode out.

AND THEN I WENT-- *HIYAH!*

YES, DEAR.

AND THEN *HIYAH!*

YES, DEAR.

AND THEN I *SQUEEZED* THE VERY LIFE FROM THE BEAST!

...

YES, DEAR.

MY LOVE, WHAT TROUBLES YOU?

I'M TIRED, IS ALL. THERE WAS AN AWFUL LOT OF HIYAH-ING AND BEASTS AND LIFE-OR-DEATH CONTESTS FOR ONE DAY.

DARLING, DON'T WORRY. I KNOW WHAT I'M DOING.

I KNOW YOU KNOW. BUT I DON'T KNOW WHAT YOU'RE DOING. OR WHERE THIS NEW LIFE WILL TAKE YOU--AND THAT TERRIFIES ME.

HERE, MY LOVE. NOW YOUR RING CARRIES SOME OF ME WITH IT.

MY CHI BLESSES IT NOW. SEE HOW IT GLOWS?

IT MEANS I AM NEAR YOU.

AND THAT I LOVE YOU.

AND THAT I STILL LIVE.

But the fisherman was still just a fisherman, thinking fisherman thoughts and dreaming dragon-less fisherman dreams.

He would **always** be a fisherman, and she would always be the **Immortal Weapon** of K'un-Lun.

Same **planet**, different **worlds**.

He would never ask her not to be who she was, but he knew in his heart he could not **take** watching her risk her life time and time again.

On that magic day that K'un-Lun intersected with the world of men, the fisherman decided to **leave**.

He could never stand between his true love and her destiny, so he would go fish elsewhere--far away from dragons and kung fu and dying of slow, sick worry.

Wu Ao-Shi found this choice **unacceptable**.

AS YOU KNOW, K'UN-LUN APPEARS IN THE WORLD OF MEN ONCE A DECADE, AND--

I WISH TO **LEAVE**.

Destiny has a way of not really caring **what** you think.

It was well within her rights to leave. It was law; it was allowed; it was her **choice**. But Yu-Ti knew in his old, bitter bones **why** she was leaving:

DO YOU WISH TO TELL ME... THAT YOU WOULD **LEAVE** THE HEAVENLY CITY AND CHOOSE **LOVE** OVER **DUTY**?

And it infuriated him.

But to Wu Ao-Shi, love and duty were one and the same.

Old, bitter men with old, bitter bones have trouble remembering that sometimes.

...WOMEN ARE INFURIATING.

So while her beloved fisherman found himself almost immediately on water-lapped shores prime for fishing...

Wu's first mistake was assuming everyone left K'un-Lun the same way, but no road out of the Heavenly City follows the same path.

Wu Ao-Shi's path was considerably more unpleasant. She always suspected this was a parting gift from Yu-Ti.

Regardless, a little snow would not stop her.

Nothing would stop her.

Lost in the world of men for the first time in her life, lost in a world where people needed **money** to **eat** and if they didn't eat, they starved...

Wu decided that, while she searched for her true love, she would do what she knew best.

She beat people up.

For money.

These were the good times.

The glory days when her legend was seeded and spread from village to village.

Things started off well for our fisherman, too. Lots of **fishing**...lots of **fish**...

But it didn't last.

Our time in Heaven is always fleeting.

Hell always stalks on its heels.

So hold onto the good times, precious ones. Hold onto those golden days.

Because you never know when **Wokou** pirates will show up, steal or burn all your earthly belongings, and **enslave you** and all of your **friends**.

Try as they might, the pirates couldn't kill **everybody**.

Eventually the news that Pinghai Bay was now in the grip of tyrant pirates spread from village to village.

And eventually it spread to the great **avenger** of the **oppressed**...

The Immortal Iron Fist. And the Immortal Iron Fist, who was now quite well-paid to beat people up, thought to herself:

$

And that was that.

Wu Ao-Shi set out for Pinghai Bay and all the tremendous wealth and violence that surely awaited her.

Arriving in Pinghai, she found it remarkably easy to enter the town undetected.

See?

And if Wu had learned anything about the world of men she now wandered, it was this:

If you want to find the head tyrant in charge, follow the flow of **loosened ladies** to his bedchamber. For surely you will find there...

The Pirate King! Felled by golden slumbers and soiled doves of easy virtue!

PIRATE KING! PINGHAI BAY IS NOW UNDER **MY RULE.**

YOU AND YOUR FLUNKIES HAVE UNTIL SUNRISE TO FLEE--LEST YOU FACE **PUNISHMENT** AT THE HANDS OF THE **IMMORTAL IRON FIST.**

CUTE, PIRATE HAREM! RID ME OF THIS **LOUD AND COMPLAINING WENCH** THAT DARED DISTURB OUR "SLEEP."

The Lessons of the Tactical Warrior, vol. 26, as written by Lei Kung the Thunderer, teaches us, "Never awaken a sleeping pirate and his boudoir army of fallen women."

But our Wu was never one for reading.

Fighting was a wholly different story.

MEN! STOP HER!

HA!

And fighting *fair* was, alas, yet a different story still.

How easy it is for Iron Fists to think that it is they themselves who are immortal...

...when it is in fact their *station* that will outlive their all-too-temporary flesh.

But Wu Ao-Shi was a **warrior**, and a hell of a warrior at that.

PIRATE **DOGS!** PREPARE TO MEET YOUR **DEATH!**

And so, her enemies fell as if **lightning from God** had destroyed them.

It was **glorious**.

KILL HER!

KILL HER **RIGHT NOW!**

SHE'S ONLY A **LITTLE GIRL!** HOW HARD CAN IT BE TO KILL A LITTLE GIRL?!

Pirates aren't much for **irony**, but Wu would later insist that be the Pirate King's **epitaph**.

How hard can it be to kill a little girl, Pirate King?

Very, very hard indeed.

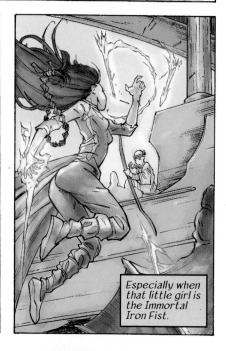

Especially when that little girl is the Immortal Iron Fist.

It continued this way for hours.

Wu would leap from her ship to one of theirs...

...beat the hell out of some pirates, **destroy** that ship, and then head **back** to her ship and lead the fleet back to land.

By the time they managed to set her junker on fire, it was too late.

She had led them too far inland and escape was impossible.

Pinghai Bay was now truly under her rule.

All that was unbeknownst to our fisherman. Being nervous, worried and otherwise uptight about the fate of his true love, he chose to do what he did best.

He fished.

And when the shores of Pinghai Bay were lapped with the ruins of his true love's enemies, he knew that this was simply how it **must be**.

And that, dear reader, was what finally set him free.

AHOY THERE, TIE ME OFF?

OF COURSE, MY LOVE.

"MY LOVE"? SO YOU FORGIVE ME MY *TRANSGRESSION*?

OF COURSE. I REALIZED THAT *YOU* COULD JUST AS SOON *STOP FIGHTING* AS I COULD STOP *PLUCKING FISH* FROM *THE SEA*.

AND WHAT TRUTH DID THIS REALIZATION BRING YOU?

WE ARE HUNGRY ALMOST EVERY SINGLE DAY.

AND IF WE ARE TO BE HUNGRY, WE SHOULD AT LEAST BE *HAPPY*.

And so they remained well fed and well loved for the rest of their days...which sadly, were not long.

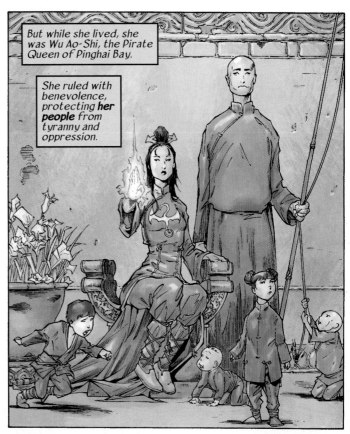

But while she lived, she was Wu Ao-Shi, the Pirate Queen of Pinghai Bay.

She ruled with benevolence, protecting **her people** from tyranny and oppression.

And she was the **last woman** ever to carry the mantle of the Iron Fist.

But the whys and the wherefores of **that** tale...

...are a story for **another** day.

THE END.

There have been sixty-six men and women to carry the mantle of THE IMMORTAL IRON FIST throughout the ages, men and women of great courage, valor, skill, and sacrifice. Sixty-six men and women have stood between man and the unstoppable forces of evil, willing to give all they have to hold back the hordes.

This is the story of one of them, as told in THE BOOK OF THE IRON FIST.

The Story of the Iron Fist Bei Bang-Wen
(1827-1860)

The Perfect Strategy Mind and his Miraculous Travels to the Dark Continent, and what Mysteries of the World and of the Self that He Learned There.

MATT FRACTION - WRITER
KHARI EVANS - PENCILER
VICTOR OLAZABA - INKER
JELENA KEVIC DJURDJEVIC &
PAUL MOUNTS - COLOR ART
DAVE LANPHEAR - LETTERER
IRENE LEE - PRODUCTION
ALEJANDRO ARBONA - ASSISTANT EDITOR
WARREN SIMONS - EDITOR
JOE QUESADA - EDITOR IN CHIEF
DAN BUCKLEY - PUBLISHER

EVEN IN HIS YOUTH, BEI BANG-WEN WAS USUALLY CONSIDERED THE SMARTEST PERSON IN THE ROOM.

AND HE **WAS**.

MOST TIMES, ANYWAY.

IT CAME AS NO SURPRISE THAT, UPON BECOMING THE **IMMORTAL IRON FIST**, BEI BANG-WEN FOUND METHODS OF USING THE **GOLDEN CHI OF SHOU-LAO THE UNDYING** IN MORE...

...CEREBRAL...

...WAYS THAN ANY OF HIS PREDECESSORS.

THIS WAS HIS PERFECT **STRATEGY MIND**, AND IT ACCOMPANIED HIM INTO EACH AND EVERY BATTLE HE FOUGHT.

AT LAST IT HAS COME TO ME!

BATTLES ARE NOT HARD FOR HIM TO FIND. IT IS 1860, AND THE ENGLISH WANT THE CHINESE TO HONOR THE TRADING TREATIES OF 1858.

IT'S NOT GOING WELL.

THE RESULT WAS WHAT WOULD EVENTUALLY BE CALLED **THE SECOND OPIUM WAR.**

THE ENGLISH AND FRENCH NAVIES HAVE CAPTURED THE PORTS OF YANTAI AND DALIAN. THE **BOHAI GULF** IS SEALED OFF.

THIS WILL END **BADLY** FOR THE CHINESE. AND THAT ENDING BEGINS HERE...

Taku Forts. 21 August 1860.

THE **PERFECT STRATEGY MIND** HAS ORCHESTRATED AN ASSAULT OF 10,000 PIECES MOVING AT ONCE IN FLAWLESS HARMONY.

EVERY MAN ON THE FORT HAS BEEN CHOREOGRAPHED WITH PRECISION.

EVERY SOLDIER KNOWS DOWN TO THE **HEARTBEAT** WHEN TO FIRE, WHEN TO MOVE, AND WHEN TO RUN.

BEI BANG-WEN BELIEVES IN THE PERFECT STRATEGY MIND.

BEI BANG-WEN BELIEVES IN THE PERFECT DEATH.

ONE WITHOUT FEAR. ONE THAT STANDS AS AN IMMORTAL TRIBUTE TO A LIFE WELL-LIVED.

BEI BANG-WEN BELIEVES THAT THIS MOMENT--HERE ABOVE THE BLOOD AND MUCK THE TAKU FORTS ARE BUILT UPON--IS THE MOMENT OF HIS DEATH.

BEI BANG-WEN IS **READY.**

BUT FOR THE FIRST TIME IN HIS LIFE...

Chapra jail. Bihar, India.

IT WOULD BE THE FIRST OF MANY.

BEI BANG-WEN WAS STRIPPED OF HIS NAME AND HIS NATIONALITY.

HE WAS STRIPPED OF HIS FREEDOMS AND HIS INDIVIDUALITY.

HE WAS BEATEN.

PROFOUNDLY AND REGULARLY, HE WAS BEATEN.

HE NEVER ONCE CURSED HIS LUCK, HIS JAILERS, OR HIS *GOD*.

HE NEVER ONCE ASKED "WHY ME?" HE NEVER PRAYED FOR DELIVERANCE, REVENGE, OR FORGIVENESS.

HE REPEATED TO HIMSELF, TIME AND TIME AGAIN, LIKE A MANTRA:

"I DESERVE *WORSE*."

OI. ON YOUR *FEET*, PRISONER.

"WORSE" WAS YET TO COME.

THIS WAS THE DAY BEI WAS INTRODUCED INTO THE LABOR GANG.

SIXTEEN HOURS A DAY, UNDER THE BEASTLY SUN, BEI WAS MADE TO LABOR WITH THE OTHER ENEMIES OF THE CROWN.

WITHOUT HIS POWERS, HE WAS A WORKER AMONGST WORKERS AND NOT A LEADER OF MEN.

BEI SOMETIMES HAD TROUBLE REMEMBERING THAT.

LET ME HELP YOU UP, MY BROTHER.

BUT IF THEY LASH ME, I INSIST YOU IMMEDIATELY RETURN THE FAVOR.

ONE THING BEI WOULD HAVE NO TROUBLE REMEMBERING WAS THE NAME OF THE MAN THAT HELPED HIM:

I AM VIVATMA VISVAJIT. HELLO.

THEY FLED.

EVERY SOUL IN CHAPRA JAIL FLED FOR THE HILLS AND FOR THEIR FAMILIES, FREE AT LAST FROM THE OPPRESSIVE THUMB OF THE BRITISH.

NOT A SINGLE ONE WAS LOST IN THE UPRISING.

AND THE TWO CHAMPIONS FLED, TOO, BUT RATHER THAN RUN TO THE HILLS OR TOWARD WHATEVER FAMILIES THEY MAY HAVE HAD--

--THEY RAN TO THE EASTERN SHORES, IN SEARCH OF A BOAT.

ONLY A BOAT COULD TAKE THEM TO BURMA.

AND BURMA WAS WHERE THE POET EMPEROR BAHADUR SHAH ZAFAR II ROTTED IN WAIT.

THE POET EMPEROR HAD MANY FANS-- INCLUDING TWO **OLD FISHERMEN** MORE THAN HAPPY TO LOAN THEIR BOAT TO THE CAUSE OF HIS FREEDOM.

AND SO OUR HEROES SET SAIL, UNITED IN THEIR MISSION.

HOW DO WE EAT?

Days later...

WE MAY HAVE MISCALCULATED SOMEWHAT.

YES. YES, WE MAY HAVE.

WE COULD USE THE ARC OF THE SEXTANT AS AN **EDGE**, GO OVERBOARD, AND USE IT TO SLASH AT A FISH, OR PERHAPS CUT AT SEAWEED.

I CAN'T SWIM.

AND SLOWLY THEY REACHED BURMA.

WASTING NO TIME, THEY WENT RACING TO FIND THEIR DESTINIES.

BEI FOLLOWED VIVATMA.

VIVATMA FOLLOWED HIS INSTINCT.

AND HIS INSTINCT WAS TRUE.

IT MIGHT AS WELL HAVE BEEN FROM OUTER SPACE.

I *REALLY* WISH I WAS STILL IN COMMUNION WITH *THE BRAHMAN.*

SURELY ONLY THE BRAHMAN COULD PENETRATE SUCH A TREMENDOUS FORTRESS.

AND SO THEY WENT.

INCH BY INCH THEY STORMED THE PALACE PRISON.

WELL.

"STORMED" MAYBE OVERSTATES THINGS.

ALL THE SAME, THEY MADE THEIR WAY INSIDE.

AND SLOWLY BUT SURELY, THEY MADE THEIR WAY UP.

EACH MAN WAS THINKING THE SAME THING BUT ALLOWING IT TO GO UNSAID BETWEEN THEM:

THIS SHOULD BE HARDER.

THERE SHOULD BE MORE GUARDS.

MORE FIGHTING.

MORE VIOLENCE.

OF COURSE IT OCCURRED TO THEM THAT THIS MUST BE A TRAP.

VIVATMA VISVAJIT BELIEVED THAT, IF IT WAS A TRAP, THEN AT LEAST HIS LORD AND MASTER WOULD BE THE BAIT.

AND BEI BANG-WEN BELIEVED THAT, IN EITHER INSTANCE, HE WOULD SOON BE DEAD.

FINALLY.

FINALLY, FINALLY, FINALLY.

WRONG AGAIN.

HUMBLING TO ONE SUCH AS BEI BANG-WEN, WHO HAD ALWAYS BELIEVED HIMSELF TO BE THE SMARTEST PERSON IN THE ROOM.

TIGER JANI WAS LONG CONSIDERED TO BE A LOCAL GHOST STORY.

A FOLK LEGEND USED BY UGLY OLD WIDOWS TO FRIGHTEN OFF THE WET-EYED DRUNKS THAT INVARIABLY WOULD COME A'COURTIN' AFTER MIDNIGHT.

TIGER JANI IS REAL?

BEI HAD FORGOTTEN WHAT IT FELT LIKE TO NOT KNOW EVERYTHING ALL THE TIME.

THAT, AND THE SUDDEN BLOOD LOSS, CREATED IN HIM A FEELING LIKE UNTO EUPHORIA.

SUDDENLY DEATH DIDN'T SEEM LIKE SUCH A GREAT IDEA.

I SHALL FEAST UPON YOUR HOLY SOULS!

OH WELL.

VIVATMA WAS STUNNED. NOT BY THE GIRL'S TRANSFORMATION--

ALTHOUGH IT WAS STUNNING--

BUT BY FINDING HIMSELF QUITE SUDDENLY WITHOUT A DIRECTION.

WITHOUT A POET EMPEROR TO SAVE, VIVATMA HAD NO PURPOSE.

WITHOUT A GREAT SIN TO ATONE FOR, VIVATMA HAD NO MORE SHAME.

AND FREE OF SHAME, VIVATMA FELT HIS KUNDALINI REALIGNING, HIS PRANA CATCHING THE MOST HOLY FIRE OF GOD IN ALL OF GOD'S GLORY.

HIS AWARENESS WAS AGAIN TRANSFORMED INTO THE INFINITE.

TIGER JANI. YOU HAVE FREED ME FROM THE PRISON OF SELF.

FOR THIS I THANK YOU.

BEI BANG-WEN HAD SEEN THINGS TO BOGGLE THE IMAGINATION.

SOMEHOW THIS TOPPED THEM ALL.

THE DAY'S EVENTS PRODUCED A KIND OF REVERIE WITHIN HIM.

TO BE TOUCHED AGAIN BY THE UNKNOWN.

THE PAST AND THE FUTURE NO LONGER EXISTING. BEI AWOKE TO FIND HIMSELF IN THE EVER-PRESENT GLORY OF THE NOW.

IT WAS WITH THIS BLISS WITHIN HIS HEART THAT HE LEAPT INTO BATTLE.

HE FOUND HIMSELF LIVING ONLY IN THE NOW.

OF FIGHTING ONLY IN THE NOW.

FREE OF THE THOUSANDS OF DEATHS HE BLAMED HIMSELF FOR, FREE OF HIS LEGACY, FREE OF HIS MISSION.

FREE.

NO--!

AND THEN HE WAS DOWN.

BEI DIDN'T EVEN FEEL IT.

HE JUST KNEW, SUDDENLY, HE WAS FALLING OVER.

THE SILENCE STARTLED THE BRAHMAN IN ITS EMPTINESS AND ENTIRE-NESS.

HIS GREAT FOE AND GREAT FRIEND WERE FELLED.

BEI BANG-WEN, MY FRIEND.

HEYYYY, FRIEND.

IT FEEEELS--

IT FEELS LIKE I'M...FLOATING AWAY.

YES.

I AM FAMILIAR WITH THE SENSATION.

LIE STILL NOW.

THE WORLDSOUL HAS BUSINESS WITH YOU YET.

THE BRAHMAN INFUSED HIS OWN PRANA TO THE HIDDEN CHI OF SHOU-LAO THAT LAY DORMANT WITHIN BEI BANG-WEN.

BEI'S CHI, NO LONGER BLOCKED BY THE FALSE BARRIERS OF SHAME AND GUILT, FLOWED WITH RENEWED INTENSITY SO GREAT--

AAAAAAAAAAHH!

--IT *HEALED* HIM.

THANK YOU.

UNBELIEVABLE!

MIRACULOUS!

I ONLY FREED WHAT WAS ALWAYS WITHIN YOU, MY BROTHER.

AND THUS DID TWO HOLY WAR DEITIES SURVIVE THEIR SELF-IMPOSED EXILE AND BETRAYAL BY *TIGER JANI.*

USING HIS PERFECT STRATEGY MIND ONCE MORE, LEI BANG-WEN DETERMINED THE WAY TO VICTORY.

VIVATMA VISVAJIT WOULD ADOPT THE ROLE OF HIS BELOVED EMPEROR, BAHADUR SHAH ZAFAR II, AND THUS WOULD HIS SUBJECTS HAVE A THING TO **BELIEVE IN**.

A HERO TO FIGHT FOR.

LEI HIMSELF WOULD RETURN TO THE GLORIOUS CITY OF HIS BIRTH.

HE COULD NOT ATONE TO THE DEAD, BUT HE COULD REJOIN THE WORLD OF THE LIVING.

HE RELINQUISHED HIS POWERS--THE CHI OF SHOU-LAO, THE MYSTICAL FORCE THAT MADE HIM THE IRON FIST--BACK INTO K'UN-LUN.

AND SO THE CYCLE OF THE IRON FIST COULD BEGIN AGAIN.

HE HAD A WIFE, AND TOGETHER THEY HAD A FAMILY OF THIRTEEN SONS.

THAT HE DIED IN THE MUD AND THE BLOOD AT THE FORTS OF TAKU REMAINS AN ESSENTIAL PART OF HIS IMMORTAL LEGEND.

THE END

ORSON
RANDALL &
THE GREEN
MIST OF
DEATH

...ero, adventurer, dashing rogue! Born and raised in the mystical city of K'un-Lun, Orson defeated the dragon Shou-Lao
...r gained extraordinary powers. With superhuman strength, speed, and fighting prowess, he became the city's Immortal
...ut after traveling to Earth and enduring the horrors of World War I, Orson refused to take part in the deadly tournament
...8 years between K'un-Lun and the six other mystical cities. Resisting his fellow Immortal Weapons' use of force, Orson
accidentally killed the Crane Champion of K'un-Zi, and fled.

...several decades — long before Danny Rand would travel to K'un-Lun and become successor to the title of the Immortal
...Orson roamed the Earth, a bounty on his head. In the company of his makeshift family, the Confederates of the Curious
...Danny's father, Wendell Rand — Orson has evaded the pursuits of the Immortal Weapons and quested around the globe
for justice and adventure as...

THE GOLDEN AGE IRON FIST!

Previously:

... — the Iron Fist and present-day Immortal Weapon of K'un-Lun — fights a war on many fronts. As the Tournament
... Cities unfolds, Danny must secure victory for K'un-Lun in order to return to Earth...and he's already lost his first
...hile the round robin elimination moves on, Danny's trainer and master, Lei Kung the Thunderer, has enlisted his aid
...n. Lei Kung is raising an army by training the women of K'un-Lun in the martial arts, and means to bring down the
city's corrupt lord. They face overwhelming odds, and defeat is all but assured.

...urnament, Danny attempted to befriend the Prince of Orphans — the oldest, most powerful and most venerated of
...mmortal Weapons — and the least known and most mysterious. But Danny was rebuffed by the enigmatic warrior.

...yway. As Lei Kung and Danny steeled themselves to launch their rebellion at dawn and rewrite the destiny of the
...ities, Danny was paid a private visit in his quarters. It was the Prince of Orphans — a.k.a. John Aman. He came to
...g the mark of the Thunderer tattooed on his chest, announcing his allegiance to their cause...and asked how Danny
...t him. Danny revealed that he'd learned of Aman by reading of the life and adventures of the Iron Fist Orson Randall,
where Aman made several appearances...

MMORTAL IRON FIST: ORSON RANDALL AND THE GREEN MIST OF DEATH

...on   **Nick Dragotta, Mike Allred and Laura Allred** Artists, Part One

Russ Heath Artist, Part Two

Lewis LaRosa, Stefano Gaudiano and Matt Hollingsworth Artists, Part Three

Mitch Breitweiser and Matt Hollingsworth Artists, Part Four

...Studios
...s

Paul Acerios Production

Alejandro Arbona Assistant Editor

Warren Simons Editor

Joe Quesada Editor in Chief

Dan Buckley Publisher

THERE'S-- AHH--I CAN SEE... UH...A WOMAN BEING UNTRUE TO HER MAN IS HERE TONIGHT...

...UM--AND, UM, TWO--TWO EMBEZZLERS. THREE BOOTLEGGERS. AND--UH...

MY WORD, I CAN SEE SO--

I CAN SEE SO MANY THINGS, LADIES AND GENTLEMEN.

I SEE... ER...I SEE...

I CAN SEE THROUGH YOU ALL...

...I CAN SEE... A LACK...

THIS MAN NEEDS HELP!

IS THERE A DOCTOR IN THE HOUSE?!?

MY WORD.

DID I PASS OUT ON STAGE?

YOU WERE *OUT COLD* LIKE CHORES AFTER PAYDAY.

HOW'RE YOU FEELIN', PAL?

HEY!

I'VE HAD BETTER NIGHTS--AND BETTER *PERFORMANCES.* I FEAR MY *PROFESSIONAL REPUTATION* HAS BEEN IRREVOCABLY *BRUISED,* NEVER TO RECOVER.

WHAT A *STRANGE MAN.*

MAN? WHAT MAN? WE THOUGHT YOU JUST NEEDED SOME O.J. AND A SUGAR COOKIE, PAL, WE DIDN'T KNOW THERE WAS A *MAN* INVOLVED.

IT WAS THE STRANGEST THING, ORSON.

I WAS USING THE *AURAL EYE OF ASMODEL* TO VIEW THE AURAS OF MY AUDIENCE, AS I ALWAYS DO...

...WHEN SITTING THERE IN THE CENTER OF THE AUDIENCE WAS ABSOLUTE NOTHINGNESS SHAPED LIKE A *MAN*...

...THEN I SAW A WHIRL OF GREEN SMOKE AND I WAS OUT COLD...

NO. THAT'S IMPOSSIBLE--NOT *HERE*--HE COULDN'T HAVE FOUND ME *HERE*--!

WHO, BOSS? YOU OKAY? YOU LOOK LIKE YOU'VE JUST SEEN A *GHOST.*

NOT A *GHOST,* WENDELL-- AN ANGEL. THE ANGEL OF *DEATH.*

JOHN AMAN IS HERE-- *THE PRINCE OF ORPHANS!*

WE JUST WALTZED INTO A TRAP AND *SHADU* HERE WAS THE BAIT.

CONFEDERATES, WHAT YOU NEED TO KNOW IS SOME VERY POWERFUL PEOPLE WANT ME *VERY DEAD* AND JOHN AMAN IS THE KIND OF GUY THAT CAN MAKE THAT HAPPEN.

SHADU, IS THERE A *SECRET PASSAGE* OUT OF HERE?

A SECRET PASSAGE? MY GOOD ORSON, THE *53RD CARD* IS AN *OCCULT SPEAKEASY.*

THERE ARE SECRET PASSAGES TO SECRET *DIMENSIONS* HERE.

DOWN THIS HALLWAY ARE DOORWAYS LEADING OUT AND AWAY FROM THIS PLACE.

THEN GO, AND DON'T LOOK *BACK.*

I THOUGHT I COULD OUTRUN HIM, BUT CLEARLY I CAN'T AND NOW YOU'RE ALL IN *GRAVE DANGER.*

WE'RE, ORSON.

WE'RE ALL IN GRAVE DANGER. YOU'RE NOT ALONE-- WHATEVER FIGHT THE PRINCE OF ORPHANS HAS WITH YOU...HE HAS WITH *ALL* OF US.

THEN *WE* ALL NEED TO *RUN LIKE HELL.* GET THE REST OF THE CONFEDERATES TO THE *DOCKS,* CONTESSA, AND I'LL--

ORSON, LOOK--!

ORSON RANDALL. AT LONG LAST.

PREPARE TO *DIE.*

YOU CANNOT OUTRUN ME FOREVER!

LIKE HELL.

FASTER, ORSON! HE'S RIGHT BEHIND YOU!

GO, DAMMIT, GO! CLOSE THE DAMN--

KSSRRRRK

HMPH.

HURRY UP, DAMMIT-- I HAD TO BRIBE THE CAPTAIN TO STAY AN EXTRA FIFTEEN MINUTES TO ACCOMMODATE YOU SLOWPOKES...

L.P., WHERE'S THE KID?

ORSON, LISTEN, ABOUT THAT...

HE TOLD ME TO TELL YOU, QUOTE, "I'M GOING AFTER THE MAGIC COINS AN' I SURE AS HELL AIN'T SCARED OF NO GREEN MIST," END QUOTE.

HE TOOK THE DOG, TOO.

DAMMIT, BOY.

FIND THE CAPTAIN, L.P.--PAY HIM TO STAY ANOTHER HOUR.

IF WE'RE NOT BACK, SET SAIL WITHOUT US.

AND YOU'LL... WHAT, RENDEZVOUS WITH US IN SINGAPORE?

NO--IF WE'RE NOT BACK IN AN HOUR, WE'LL BE DEAD.

WENDELL?

I COULDN'T JUST LEAVE THE COINS, ORSON. I COULDN'T.

WENDELL, DAMMIT, AMAN IS ON TO US--THERE'S NO TIME FOR--

I AIN'T CHICKEN, ORSON. I AIN'T RUNNING.

IT'S NOT THAT SIMPLE, BOY--

THE HELL IT AIN'T.

TOLD YOU A MILLION TIMES--"ISN'T," NOT "AIN'T."

HEY.

I DON'T CARE, YA BIG COWARD. IF YOU THINK I'M GONNA--

IF YOU THINK--

WENDELL. LISTEN TO ME.

WE'RE NOT READY FOR A FIGHT THIS SIZE. WE'RE NOT READY FOR A FOE THIS *GREAT*.

AND AS LONG AS YOU AND THE REST OF THE CONFEDERATES RUN WITH ME, I HAVE TO PUT YOUR SAFETY FIRST.

AW, THAT'S GARBAGE AND YOU KNOW IT, ORSON.

YOU TAUGHT ME TO NEVER RUN AWAY FROM A FIGHT, NEVER EVER. SO I *DON'T*--AND NOW YOU'RE TELLING ME THAT'S WHAT WE NEED TO DO?

I AIN'T-- I'M *NOT*--AFRAID, ORSON.

I KNOW, SON. I KNOW.

BUT YOU *SHOULD* BE.

BESIDES, THE COINS ARE JUST-- THEY'RE BAUBLES, WEND, THEY DON'T MEAN ANYTHING.

EASY FOR YOU TO SAY! THEY'RE FROM *MAGICAL CITIES* THAT AIN'T EVEN *ON EARTH!* THEY MIGHT BE JUNK TO YOU, BUT TO ME THEY'RE--

BARK BARK

BOSS. LOOK!

DAMMIT.

"HNN.

"NICE WORK BACK THERE, KID.

"YOU ALMOST GOT YOURSELF KILLED FOR A HANDFUL OF *COINS*."

I *TOLD YOU*, BOSS, TO ME THEY'RE--

--THEY'RE MAGICAL, BOSS. ALL MY LIFE I BEEN BEAT UP AND HALF-STARVED AND LUCKY NOT TO DIE IN SOME GUTTER SOMEWHERE, AND THESE COINS YOU GAVE ME--

--THEY'RE THE PROMISE OF A *BETTER LIFE*, OF BIGGER THINGS'N I RIGHTLY DESERVE.

THAT'S MY *DESTINY*, BOSS-- AND NO SUPER-POWERED CREEP LIKE JOHN AMAN IS GONNA KEEP ME FROM IT.

I'M PLAYING FOR *KEEPS*.

LESSON NUMBER ONE, KID-- JOHN AMAN WON'T REST UNTIL HE FINDS ME, AND THAT MEANS THE LIVES OF THE *CONFEDERATES OF THE CURIOUS* ARE ON THE LINE. THIS AIN'T NO *GAME*.

"*ISN'T*," BOSS. THIS *ISN'T* A GAME.

SHUT UP, BOY...

WE'D EXPECT NOTHING LESS FROM ONE OF THE "CONFEDERATES OF THE CURIOUS."

PIGS.

OPPRESSORS!

YOU--

--YOU'RE THEM LASSES FROM THE *SALOON* LAST NIGHT--

SILENCE!

AAAGH--!

YOU FELL INTO THE OLDEST *TRAP* IN THE BOOK, YOU DRUNKEN IRISH GOON--

--THE *HONEY* TRAP--

--AND NOW WE JUST KEEP YOU HERE LONG ENOUGH TO COLLECT OUR BOUNTY...

...FROM *JOHN AMAN,* THE *PRINCE OF ORPHANS.*

HE'S COMING FOR YOU, CHORES MacGILLICUDDY. AND MORE IMPORTANTLY...

ORSON RANDALL!

ARE YOU... ACTUALLY *GROOMING*?

Y'KNOW, CONTESSA, I ALWAYS PROMISED MY MOMMA I'D LOOK *GOOD* ON THE DAY I DIED.

I THOUGHT YOUR MOTHER *DIED* IN CHILDBIRTH.

MAYBE SHE *DID.*

WENDELL! QUIT PRACTICING YOUR KUNG FU AND GET THESE HORSES LOADED UP.

HI-YAHH!

SUCH MENIAL LABOR IS BENEATH ONE SUCH AS I--

THE IMMORTAL IRON FIST!

DAMMIT, WENDELL--I *TOLD* YOU--

YOU'RE NOT IRON FIST. YOU'RE NOT GONNA *BE* IRON FIST. AND THE SOONER YOU GET THAT DAMN FOOL IDEA OUT OF YOUR HEAD--

--THE LONGER YOU'LL LIVE. GOT IT?

GOT IT. *JERK.*

GOOD. NOW ALL OF YOU, *GET READY* FOR ACTION.

CHORES WAS *WELL IN HIS CUPS* WHEN WE LEFT HIM LAST NIGHT, AND SINCE HE DIDN'T MAKE IT BACK TO CAMP...

I EXPECT THINGS ARE GOING TO GET *REAL EXCITING* DOWN THERE REAL *FAST.*

My name is Orson Randall. Once upon a time...

...I was the Immortal Iron Fist. But now I'm just a man...

...and I just want to take care of my friends, not cause any **trouble,** and live a quiet life.

I'D LIKE TO BAIL MY FRIEND OUT AND NEVER DARKEN YOUR DOORSTEP AGAIN.

MA'AM.

WELL, WELL, WELL.

NEVER THOUGHT I'D LIVE TO HEAR THE LEGENDARY ORSON RANDALL *BEG.*

ORSON? OH MY GOD, IS *ORSON* OUT THERE?

SHUT UP--

ORSON, IT'S A TRAP! IT'S *AMAN!*

JOHN AMA≋

DAMMIT.

MA'AM, I'D STEP AWAY FROM THAT DOOR IF I WERE YOU...

LOOKS AS THOUGH ORSON'S HOSPITALITY HAS BEEN WELCOMED AS PER *USUAL*, CONTESSA--YOU DON'T NEED THE HOARY HOSTS OF HOGGOTH TO TELL YOU *THAT*.

INDEED, SHADU.

CONFEDERATES-- LET'S RIDE.

COWGIRLS FROM HELL--TAKE HIM D...

GIRLS, GIRLS, GIRLS--

I'M REALLY NOT INTERESTED IN ANYTHING *SERIOUS* RIGHT NOW.

GET 'EM, BOSS!

GO AHEAD AND *JOKE*, RANDALL.

NO ONE CAN SAVE YOU NOW.

OH, I DUNNO ABOUT THAT...

"...I HAVE SOME PRETTY DETERMINED FRIENDS."

DON'T SHOOT UNTIL YOU SEE THE WHITES OF THEIR THIGHS!

SALOON

C'MON, CONFEDERATES--!

SHOW THEM LADYKILLIN' LADY-KILLERS WHAT FOR!

BWOCKA-BWOCKA-BWOCKA

SOMETHING'S NOT RIGHT--

URK--

RED...?

MY LORD--

HRRG. HRRRRRG. HRRRKKKK---

HA HA HA HA HA HA...

OUR FORMER MASTERS HAVE SET ME TO RECOVERING STOLEN PROPERTY OF THEIRS THAT LIES IN YOUR POSSESSION. SEVEN SACRED COINS, ONE FROM *EACH* OF HEAVEN'S SEVEN CAPITAL CITIES.

OOOOHHH...

ALL OF YOU.

GET THE HELL OUT OF HERE.

ALL OF YOU.

ORSON, I--

SO IT'S NOT JUST ORSON RANDALL, MURDERER, THAT I HUNT-- BUT ORSON RANDALL, *THIEF.*

GIVE ME THE COINS AND I'LL SPARE THEM AS CIVILIANS, RATHER THAN YOUR ALLIES.

HA!

GRRAHH--

KII!

KRAK

DAMN FOOL'LL GET HIMSELF KILLED--

AN' I DIDN'T SPEND FIFTEEN YEARS AS NO *CIRCUS STRONGMAN* TO LET A DUMB DAMN *CAGE* STOP ME FROM SAVING MY PALS--

ALMOST-- ALLLLMOST--

OUR KIND HAS A *CODE*, RANDALL. YOU USING YOUR *FRIENDS* AS HUMAN SHIELDS *VIOLATES* THAT CODE.

I AM NOT *EVIL*, RANDALL, NO MATTER WHAT YOU MAY THINK OF ME.

WHEN YOU ALLOWED YOUR FRIENDS TO GET INVOLVED IN THIS WAR BETWEEN THE IMMORTAL WEAPONS, YOU PUT THEM ALL IN DANGER.

FROM THIS POINT ON, AS LONG AS THEY STAND WITH YOU, YOUR CRIMES ARE THEIR CRIMES...AS ARE YOUR *PUNISHMENTS*...

...*TEND* TO YOUR WOUNDED, AND MAKE YOUR DECISION. ARE YOU MAN ENOUGH TO STAND ALONE AGAINST ME, ORSON RANDALL?

JAYSIS, MARY AND JOSEPH IN HEAVEN!

WAS I DEAD? WHAT *HAPPENED?*

HE'LL GIVE US UNTIL *SUNUP*, THEN START HUNTING AGAIN. BUT HE'S RIGHT--I CAN'T RISK THE LIVES OF MY FRIENDS WHILE THEY FIGHT MY FIGHTS ANY LONGER.

THE *CONFEDERATES OF THE CURIOUS* ARE FINISHED...

"...AND IT'LL BE A COLD DAY IN *HELL* THAT YOU AND I FACE EACH OTHER AGAIN..."

RANDALL! ORSON *RANDALL!*

DAMMIT, MAN-- I JUST HUNTED AND SLAUGHTERED THE MIDNIGHT MIGOU OF THE PRECIPICE PERILOUS--≥HIC≥--

--SO UNLESS YOU'RE COMIN' BY TO INQUIRE AS TO THE ROOM TO LET--

--YOU BEST LET ME DRINK MYSELF TO DEATH IN *PEACE.*

THIS *TELEGRAM,* SIR-- IT CAME FROM *FRANCE!*

SOMEWHERE IN PARIS, YOUR *FATHER* IS ON HIS *DEATHBED!*

THE END

16

THE PARTNER

THE FRIEND

THE LOVER

THE
IMMORTAL
IRON
FIST

They move as one.

Just like they've been trained.

WHAT ARE YOU WAITING FOR? YOUR MOMMY NEED TO SIGN A PERMISSION SLIP?

LET'S *GO*.

The goading doesn't shake them off their game.

Whatever edge I was hoping the **trash talk** might buy me...

Negligible at best.

Now there's nothing left to do but get a little **bloodied**...

COME ON!

They charge.

Fearlessly, relentlessly...they come at me...

The **Thunder Dojo** teaches its students no less.

I couldn't be prouder of them.

"Happy Birthday Danny"

Matt Fraction — Writer
David Aja — Art
Matt Hollingsworth — Color Art
Dave Lanphear — Letterer
Alejandro Arbona — Assistant Editor
Warren Simons — Editor
Joe Quesada — Editor in Chief
Dan Buckley — Publisher

The space was apparently an old furniture warehouse that **Rand International** had acquired somewhere along the line, up in **Harlem.**

It's in the heart of a neighborhood that's seen better days.

And it's a neighborhood full of kids...

...almost all of 'em needing a place like the **Dojo** to come after school.

We have tutors, too, to help 'em with schoolwork.

The better the grades, the more **privileges** they get.

Thirteen million-some hungry kids in this country. Although the government doesn't call it "hungry." The government calls it being "food insecure."

Being "food insecure" ruins health, raises infection rates, creates **psychosocial** issues, causes problems with aggression, and absolutely runs riot over academic performance.

So here, everybody eats.

And meditates.

Meditation increases blood flow, concentration, and lowers stress. All things these kids need; all things these kids can **use.**

Hell, after the last few months, I can use it, too.

SENSEI DANNY...?

Namely *gutting* it and *shutting it down.*

Multinational conglomerates are almost impossible to kill, as it turns out. Dismantling it piece by piece can take forever.

I found out the root of my family's fortune was the **Randall fortune**...

...and the Randall fortune was rooted in the blood and oppression of the people of not just K'un-Lun, but of all of the **Capital Cities of Heaven**...

So I'm giving it away.

Every blood-soaked dime.

I'm turning **Rand** into the world's largest and most deeply funded not-for-profit charitable organization.

I'll spend the rest of my life doing my best to die broke.

Transforming us from this into that, though...

...means there's a whole lot of **changes** happening on every level.

WHAT *DEPARTMENT* DID THIS USED TO BE, DANNY?

I THINK THIS WAS *ACQUISITIONS*, RIGHT?

IT WAS EITHER *MERGERS* OR ACQUISITIONS.

Jeryn Hogarth. The man that ran the company, for all intents and purposes. Its primary operations officer.

My mentor.

And friend.

ACQUISITIONS.

MERGERS WAS ON *EIGHT.* I KNOW BECAUSE WE *BLEW IT UP* WHEN XAO AND DAVOS ATTACKED.

COST A FORTUNE TO BUILD ALL THOSE CUSTOM DESKS.

EH. WE'LL REBUILD 'EM ALL AGAIN IN THE *NEW* HEADQUARTERS.

YEAH.

ABOUT THAT, DANNY...

I NEED TO *GO.*

DAVOS AND XAO DIDN'T JUST BLOW UP *MERGERS,* DANNY. THEY HURT MY *MOM.*

AND I KNOW WHAT YOU'RE WORKING TOWARD THESE DAYS AND... AND IT'S NOT FOR ME ANYMORE.

I ADMIRE THE HELL OUT OF WHAT YOU'RE DOING, DANNY-- GIVING IT ALL AWAY AND ALL THAT.

I KNOW IT WASN'T LONG AGO I GAVE YOU A HARD TIME BECAUSE YOU WERE FEELING A LITTLE MORE *BILL GATES* THAN *BONO.*

BUT I'VE ALWAYS BEEN A *BUILDER.* I CAN'T STICK AROUND AND DISMANTLE THE SHOP.

THERE'LL BE A YOU-SHAPED HOLE HERE WITHOUT YOU.

YOU WERE THE HEART AND SOUL OF THIS PLACE, JERYN.

NO I WASN'T, DANNY. YOU WERE. YOU *ALWAYS* WERE.

...

I WAS THE BRAINS.

YEAH, DANNY, IT'S TIME FOR ME TO MOVE ON. BE WITH MOM, FIGURE THINGS OUT.

YOU HEADED ALL THE WAY DOWN?

NO.

I NEED TO STOP ON *13* FIRST.

13?

DANNY, THERE'S NO 13TH FLOOR.

STAY IN *TOUCH*, JERYN.

He's right, in a way. In the elevators, the stairwells, even in the plans on file with the city--

The *Rand Tower* has no 13th floor.

DANIEL.

WE HAVE NEWS.

But I've always loved *secrets*...

YEAH? HAVE YOU FOUND THE **EIGHTH CITY?**

The Iron Fist is the **Immortal Weapon** of the mystical city of K'un-Lun...one of **seven weapons,** from one of **seven cities,** that each appear on Earth in an arcane celestial sequence.

John Aman-- the Prince of Orphans.

Me.

Bride of Nine Spiders.

Fat Cobra.

Tiger's beautiful daughter.

Dog Brother #1.

We Weapons were made to combat each other in a dimension-spanning kung fu tournament.

A madman named Xao tried to destroy K'un-Lun, and the other cities, until we joined together and fought him back.

WE CANNOT PROVE IT A **LIE.**

Before he died...Xao spoke of an **eighth** city.

THAT'S YOUR NEWS? WE CAN'T PROVE IT **DOESN'T** EXIST?

It has...**vexed us**...to put it mildly.

Some of the Weapons left their homes and returned to New York, with me, to seek the city out...

...although I suspect some of them just wanted to spend a little time here.

DANNY RAND! JOIN US IN THE SCOURING OF THESE MANY SCROLLS!

ALREADY I HAVE LEARNED SEVERAL **LOST LANGUAGES** AND OF SEVERAL FASCINATING **MYTH CYCLES!**

Nevertheless, we've been searching...

YOU SEE, IF WE CANNOT OUTRIGHT PROVE HE'S LYING, THEN THAT PRESENTS US WITH THE VERY REAL CHANCE THAT XAO WAS TELLING THE TRUTH.

WE'VE TRACED XAO'S FAMILIAL LINEAGE BACK TO *THE LIGHTNING LORDS OF NEPAL.*

I TANGLED WITH THEM FROM TIME TO TIME, AS DID, I BELIEVE, YOUR PREDECESSOR.

THE THREE XAO BROTHERS COULD COMBINE THEIR CHI TO CREATE A KIND OF *BEAST* MADE OF *PURE LIGHTNING.*

WE HAVE REASON TO BELIEVE ORSON RANDALL *KILLED* ONE OF THE BROTHERS.

IT LOOKS LIKE *YOUR PREDECESSOR* EMPLOYED XAO, IF I'M READING THIS RIGHT. USED HIM AS A BOUNTY HUNTER TO HUNT *DOWN* ORSON.

DID THE PREVIOUS *BRIDE* EVER MENTION--

AAH--

III KNOW WHAAAT DAY ITTT ISSS, DANNNIEL RANNND.

OHHHHH-KAY. THAT WAS CREEPY.

KEEP DIGGING. I'LL BE BACK *SOON.*

I HAVE A MEETING ACROSS TOWN I HAVE TO GET TO. BIG MEETING. *CRAZY* IMPORTANT.

FIG NEWTONS.

AND SOME-- SOME ORANGE JUICE.

I WOULD ACTUALLY *KILL* A GUY FOR FIG NEWTONS AND SOME ORANGE JUICE.

≥HEFF≥

OUT OF PRACTICE.

BOTH OF US.

WE HAD SOME STUFF, Y'KNOW?

IT GETS IN THE WAY SOMETIMES.

AIN'T THAT THE BITCH OF IT ALL, DANNY RAND?

ALL THAT STUFF, GETTIN' IN THE WAY.

...

WHAT ARE WE *DOING*, MISTY? YOU AND ME.

WHAT ARE WE DOING? WHAT *ARE* WE?

WE'RE *COMPLICATED.*

MAYBE I DON'T WANT TO BE COMPLICATED ANYMORE.

OR MAYBE I JUST CAN'T TAKE ANY MORE COMPLICATIONS, I DON'T KNOW.

LOOK, THIS THING-- THE IRON FIST--IT'S NOT A *JOB,* IT'S NOT A HOBBY. IT'S NOT FANTASY BASEBALL AND IT'S NOT A THING I DO WITH MY PALS ON WEEKENDS--

IT'S AS MUCH WHO I AM AS BEING... *BEING YOU* IS A PART OF YOU.

IT GETS IN THE WAY. OF THE HUMAN STUFF. I KNOW THAT, YOU KNOW THAT. OKAY.

WHAT I'M SAYING IS--IF WE KNOW THAT, ISN'T THAT AS BAD AS IT GETS? ISN'T THAT AS *COMPLICATED?*

I'M TIRED OF BEING WITH YOU BETWEEN THE MOMENTS OF MY LIFE.

SO WHAT *ARE* WE, MISTY? WHAT ARE WE *DOING?* WE'RE EITHER YOU AND ME, OR--OR WE'RE NOT.

YOU TELL ME.

LET ME THINK ABOUT IT.

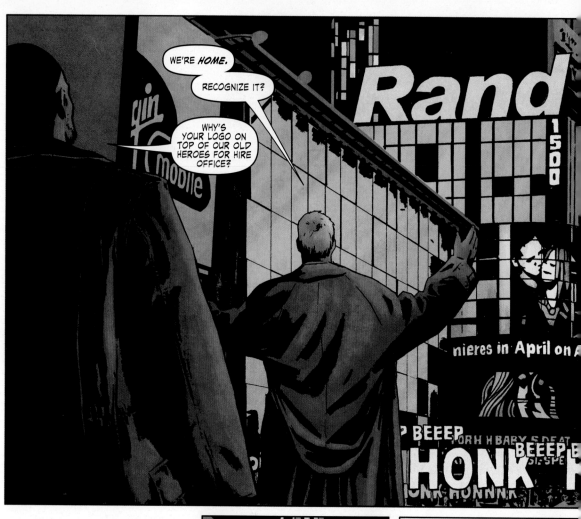

WE'RE *HOME.*

RECOGNIZE IT?

WHY'S YOUR LOGO ON TOP OF OUR OLD HEROES FOR HIRE OFFICE?

BECAUSE I BOUGHT IT. IT *WAS* A THEME RESTAURANT WHERE MODELS WHO WERE DRESSED UP LIKE HOCKEY PLAYERS SCHLEPPED TWENTY-TWO-DOLLAR BURGERS, BUT NOW IT'S-- IT'S MY NEW--

IT'S *OUR* NEW HEADQUARTERS. WORK FOR ME. WORK *WITH* ME.

DANNY, I'M A FUGITIVE, THE AVENGERS ARE--

HONK HONNNK
HONNNNK HONK BEEEP BEE
HONK HONNNK

WE'LL WORK IT OUT, MAN. WE *ALWAYS* WORK IT OUT.

LUKE, LISTEN TO ME FOR A SECOND--

I HAVE BILLIONS OF DOLLARS-- *BILLIONS*, LUKE-- THAT I'M GONNA SPEND THE REST OF MY LIFE GIVING AWAY.

COME ON. LET'S SEE WHAT HAPPENS TO THE WORLD'S PROBLEMS WHEN WE THROW CRAPLOADS OF MONEY AT THEM.

DANNY... SLOW DOWN, MAN. DEEP BREATHS.

HOW MUCH *SLEEP* ARE YOU GETTING THESE DAYS?

DO YOU EVEN KNOW WHAT *DAY* IT IS?

THE CHI OF SHOU-LAO, THE TECHNIQUES I'VE ACQUIRED--

WAIT, WAS THAT A RHETORICAL QUESTION?

LUKE, BUDDY, I LOVE YOU. WITH EVERY FIBER OF MY BEING, YOU KNOW THAT.

AND WHEN WE WORKED HERE, BACK IN THE DAY--

--THOSE WERE SOME OF THE BEST DAYS OF MY LIFE.

FIRST HONEST DAY OF WORK I EVER DID, I DID FOR YOU. BACK WHEN THIS WAS *THE DEUCE* AND NOT DISNEY'S NEW YORK, NEW YORK--

WE DID A LOT OF GOOD *HELPING PEOPLE*, MAN. REAL PEOPLE, WITH REAL PROBLEMS.

AND THE AVENGERS STUFF IS GREAT--I LOVE, Y'KNOW, FIGHTING *KANG* AND STUFF WITH YOU GUYS. I DON'T WANT TO STOP THAT.

BUT ASK A FAMILY THAT LIVES UNDER A BRIDGE ABOUT KANG, AND THEY JUST WANT THEIR KID TO EAT TONIGHT, Y'KNOW?

WORK WITH ME. LET THE NEW *RAND* CUT YOU A PAYCHECK, AND LET'S SPEND SOME TIME ON THE STREET HELPING REAL FOLKS GET BY AGAIN.

BESIDES, THE DAMN BUILDING COST ME A FORTUNE TO BUY BACK. I'M GONNA FEEL LIKE AN IDIOT IF I'M IN THERE ALONE.

ALL RIGHT, PARTNER. ALL RIGHT.

I never get around to telling him that I don't sleep much at all anymore.

I've got too much to do these days...

It started off as a veterans' outreach.

But then you get down to the homeless camps and--well, how do you tell one guy he gets some food because he served, and another guy he doesn't because he didn't?

Surviving everything--the attack on Rand, Xao, the kung fu tournament... all of it just brought the rest of my life into focus.

So a few times a week we load up the van and go around to the homeless camps.

It seems, quite literally some nights, like the absolute least I can do.

I'm the scion of a centuries-spanning kung fu dynasty and a billionaire.

Sometimes my notion of helping people can get pretty abstract.

This...helps keep me grounded.

...but a **family** that welcomes me if I just reach out to them.

A history that aches to teach.

And I am its most eager student.

I barely remember a time when I didn't feel like an orphan, an **outworlder,** a tourist, or an impostor.

But now...

...I'm a link in a chain extending backwards through time **and** forwards simultaneously.

I have never been **more** of who and what I am than I am...

...right now.

The **Book of the Iron Fist** tethers me to a world greater than myself.

And in its pages, I am **home.** I am **safe**--

WHOA.

WAIT.

C'MON C'MON C'MON--

--DAMMIT. NO.

NO NO NO NO--

Stupid--

Stupid, stupid--

How could I have missed this before? How could I not have **caught this**--?

Every Iron Fist--

--every **single one**--

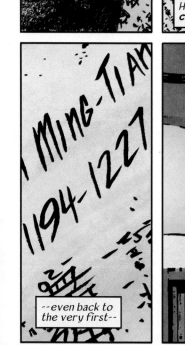

--even back to the very first--

They've all **died** at **thirty-three**.

The same age Orson was when he went **missing**.

DANNY...?

HAPPY BIRTHDAY, DANNY!

WHAT ARE YOU WAITING FOR?

MAKE A *WISH*, BABY. A BIG ONE.

MAKE IT *COUNT.*

THE IMMORTAL IRON FIST

THE ORIGIN OF DANNY RAND

Framing Sequence
Writer: Matt Fraction
Artist: Kano
Letterer: Dave Lanphear

Chapter 1: "The Fury of Iron Fist"
Writer: Roy Thomas
Penciler: Gil Kane

Chapter 2: "Heart of the Dragon"
Writer: Len Wein
Penciler: Larry Hama

Inker: Dick Giordano
Colorist: Sotocolor's A. Crossley
Letterer: L.P. Gregory

Cover Artists: Gil Kane, Larry Hama & Rain Beredo

Special Thanks to Warren Simons & Alejandro Arbona

Editor: Jeff Youngquist
Assistant Editor: Cory Levine
Production: Spring Hoteling & Nelson Ribeiro
Select Art Reconstruction: Tom Smith
Senior Vice President of Sales: David Gabriel

Editor in Chief: Joe Quesada
Publisher: Dan Buckley

DO YOU REMEMBER WHAT THE FIRST WORDS I SAID TO YOU WERE?

OF COURSE I DO.

YOU SAID "OKAY, ZORRO," AND TRIED TO PUNCH ME IN THE HEAD.

WHAT?

IT'S TRUE! YOU DID. THEN WE SCRAPPED A LITTLE AND I KNOCKED YOU OUT AND KEPT DOING...

I DUNNO, WHATEVER THE HELL IT WAS I WAS DOING.

GOD, THAT WAS A CRAZY TIME.

I'LL SAY.

SEEMS LIKE IT WAS A MILLION YEARS AGO, Y'KNOW?

YEAH, EVERYTHING'S DIFFERENT NOW.

HELL, JUST LOOK AT TIMES SQUARE-- IT LOOKS LIKE DISNEYWORLD NOW, BUT THEN--

"--IT MIGHT AS WELL HAVE BEEN ANOTHER PLANET."

IT MUST'VE BEEN--

COMING FROM K'UN-LUN, DID YOU--

WHAT WAS IT *LIKE* FOR YOU, BACK THEN? WHAT WAS IT LIKE TO SHOW UP IN NEW YORK CITY FROM OUT OF NOWHERE?

IT WAS--

OVERWHELMING. PURE AND TOTAL SENSORY OVERLOAD. SO MUCH OF MY TIME IN K'UN-LUN WAS SPENT TRAINING AND WORKING AND MEDITATING...

SOMETIMES IT FELT LIKE MY MIND JUST *SHUT DOWN* TO BLOCK IT ALL OUT AND PROTECT ME.

IT'S AMAZING YOU REMEMBER ANYTHING AT ALL.

OH, I REMEMBER.

I REMEMBER *EVERYTHING.*

...NOR WILL ANY ONE OF THEM SOON *RISE* AGAIN.

IT HAS ALL TAKEN BUT A *MINUTE*, PERHAPS, AS MEN MEASURE TIME-- A *SINGLE* MINUTE, DURING WHICH YOU MUST HAVE SEEMED AN *INHUMAN* FIGHTING-MACHINE.

BUT NOW, THE BEADS OF PERSPIRATION WHICH DOT THE *DRAGON BRAND* ON YOUR CHEST REMIND YOU THAT YOU ARE, AFTER ALL, MERELY A *MAN.*

PERHAPS THAT IS *ENOUGH.*

STANDING UPRIGHT, THOUGH BREATHING HARD, YOU ADDRESS AT LAST THE *AUGUST PERSONAGE OF JADE...*

O *YÜ-TI*--O FATHER-HEAVEN, AND LORD OF THE *K'UN-LUN MOUNTAIN*--I HAVE FACED THE *CHALLENGE OF THE MANY,* AND I HAVE *PREVAILED.*

I STAND READY NOW TO MEET THE *CHALLENGE OF THE ONE!*

THEN *STAND,* MY SON... STAND AND *THINK.*

IT IS NOT *MEET* THAT ONE SHOULD GO, PERHAPS, TO HIS *DEATH...*WITHOUT FIRST A MOMENT'S *CONTEMPLATION.*

THINK, HOODED ONE? OF *WHAT?* OF *WHOM?*

OF *YOURSELF,* MY SON,...AND OF THOSE THINGS WHICH HAVE *BROUGHT* YOU TO THIS *DAYS OF DAYS...!*

THINK, I SAY!

AND SO, *CLOSING* YOURSELF TO OUTSIDE EVENTS, YOU *DO* THINK...

AND YOU *SEE,* WITH A MIND'S EYE MORE CLEAR THAN ANY SEAMAN'S GLASS:

YOU SEE... *YOURSELF.*

YOURSELF, AS YOU *WERE.*

IT WAS ALMOST EXACTLY *TEN* YEARS AGO...

...WHEN *FOUR BLACK SPECKS* MADE THEIR *TRACKLESS* WAY ACROSS THE SNOW-CRUSTED *ASIAN WASTES.*

YOU WERE A LAD OF *NINE,* THEN,... AND YOU DIDN'T KNOW *WHY* YOU WERE THERE, THOUGH YOU WERE SOON TO *LEARN.*

OTHERS SEEMED TO KNOW LITTLE MORE THAN *YOU.*

...WENDELL, IF OUR *FACTORY-WORKERS* COULD SEE US NOW, THEY'D THINK WE WERE *ALL CRAZY!*

PERHAPS YOU'RE *RIGHT,* HAROLD...

YOU, FOR SCOURING HALF THE *HIMALAYAS,* IN SEARCH OF YOUR OWN MAD VERSION OF *SHANGRI-LA* ...

...YOUR *WIFE* AND *CHILD,* FOR ALLOWING THEMSELVES TO BE *DRAGGED ALONG...*

...AND *I,* MOST OF ALL, FOR NOT STAYING IN *NEW YORK,* WHERE THE WORST THING THAT COULD HAPPEN TO ME MIGHT BE A *STALLED LIMOUSINE* IN WINTER *!*

IN FACT, I'LL NEVER UNDERSTAND *WHY*, AFTER YOU FAILED TO TALK ME OUT OF BRINGING *HEATHER* AND *DANNY*...

...*WHY* I ENDED UP *TRAILING ALONG*, AFTER ALL?

WHERE'S THE *MYSTERY?* WE'RE *BUSINESS PARTNERS*, AREN'T WE-- *RAND & MEACHUM* --

-- AND *FRIENDS*, TO BOOT!

WHAT ARE FRIENDS *FOR*, IF NOT TO INDULGE EACH OTHER'S *DELUSIONS?*

I KNOW I *INSISTED* ON COMING, WENDELL--BUT IF ONLY IT WEREN'T SO *COLD!* AND THE *WIND*--!

IT BLOWS US THE SILENT MUSIC OF THE *K'UN-LUN MOUNTAIN*, DARLING...IF ONLY YOU OTHERS COULD *HEAR* IT, AS *I* CAN.

SOMETIMES... I THINK *I* HEAR IT, DAD.

DO YOU, SON?

DEAREST HEATHER...PLEASE... JUST BEAR WITH ME A LITTLE WHILE *LONGER...*

WE'LL *REACH OUR GOAL*...AND EVERYTHING WILL BE *CLEAR* TO YOU, AT LAST!

WHEREVER *YOU* GO, MY DARLING..!

AND WE'D *BETTER* GO--*NOW!*

EVEN AS A CHILD, YOU KNEW YOUR FATHER HAD ALWAYS BEEN AN ENIGMA TO EVERYONE:

APPEARING OUT OF *NOWHERE*, NEARLY A DECADE BEFORE-- BECOMING AN INSTANT *ENTREPRENEUR*, WITH MYSTERIOUS FUNDS --

--EVEN WINNING YOUR MOTHER'S *HAND*-- YOUR MOTHER, ONCE THE *BELLE* OF NEW YORK SOCIETY.

BUT THIS WAS *DIFFERENT*--THIS SEARCH FOR THE *K'UN-LUN MOUNTAIN*, THE MYTHICAL DWELLING-PLACE OF THE *IMMORTALS*, IN CHINESE LEGEND.

IN OLD TALES, THE MOUNTAIN LIES AT *EARTH'S CENTER*. BUT YOUR FATHER SEEMED CONVINCED IT WAS SITUATED IN *ASIA* ITSELF...

...THAT IT UNDERLAY SUCH COLORFUL VISIONS AS *SHANGRI-LA*, WHICH THE WORLD THOUGHT A CREATION OF *FICTION*.

PERHAPS YOU WERE THINKING OF THESE THINGS EVEN AS YOU TOOK A *MISSTEP* CROSSING A DEEP GORGE--AND PULLED YOUR MOTHER *BEHIND* YOU!

HEATHER! DANNY!

EEEEE!!

THEN, OUR COMBINED WEIGHT PULLED OVER YOUR FATHER, AS WELL.

THE NEXT MOMENT, THE ROPE THAT HELD THE THREE OF YOU TOGETHER SNAPPED--LEAVING YOUR FATHER DANGLING PRE-CARIOUSLY FROM THE NATURAL BRIDGE--

--AND YOU AND YOUR MOTHER ROLLING OVER AND OVER AGAIN, DOWN THE SNOW-PACKED MOUNTAINSIDE.

SOMEHOW, THE TWO OF YOU CAME TO REST ON A LEDGE NOT FAR BE-LOW, YOUR MOTHER STUNNED BY THE IMPACT FROM WHICH SHE HAD MANAGED TO SHIELD YOU.

HAROLD! PULL ME UP-- FAST!

THEN, AS YOU GAZED AT HER, FORLORN AND SHOCKED, YOU HEARD SOUNDS FROM FAR ABOVE...

WE'VE GOT TO GET--ANOTHER ROPE! THROW IT TO HEATHER-- AND DANNY!

WH-WHY ARE YOU STARING AT ME THAT WAY, MAN? FOR GOD'S SAKE-- DO SOME-THING!!

OH, I'LL DO SOME-THING ALL RIGHT, OLD FRIEND...

...BUT I DON'T THINK YOU'RE GOING TO LIKE IT!

YOUR FATHER WAS A STRONG MAN... STRONG IN BODY, STRONG OF WILL.

IT TOOK LONG SECONDS FOR THE CRUSHING PRESSURE OF HAROLD MEACHUM'S BOOT TO LOOSEN HIS GRIP ON THE ICE-COLD ROCK.

BUT, AT LAST, YOUR FATHER FELL.

WENDELL! OH MY GOD-- WENDELL!!

PERHAPS YOU KNEW, EVEN THEN, THAT YOU'D SEE THAT HORRIBLE SIGHT *AGAIN* AND *AGAIN*, EVERY NIGHT OF YOUR *LIFE*...

AND ALWAYS, THE DREAM WOULD END THE *SAME* WAY.

WITH A MUFFLED, THROAT-CAUGHT *SOB* FROM THE HUSBAND-LESS WOMAN BEHIND YOU.

THEN, A *VOICE* INTRUDED ONCE MORE UPON YOUR OWN PRIVATE *HELL*...

AND YOU WONDERED *WHY* I ACCOMPANIED YOU, WENDELL RAND?

WELL, NOW THERE IS *NO MORE* MEACHUM & RAND-- ONLY RAND, INC.--

-- AND NO ONE WILL EVER BE ABLE TO PROVE I *KILLED* YOU!

EXHILARATION WAS SWEEPING OVER HAROLD MEACHUM...EXHILARATION, AND A SENSE OF *POWER*...

--WHEN THE FIRST *ROCK* STRUCK AND BLOODIED HIS CHEEK.

THUK!

PERHAPS THAT IS WHY HE LOOKED MORE *SHOCKED* THAN TRULY *HURT*--

BUT STILL, THERE WAS FIERY HATRED IN THE HAND THAT FLUNG IT.

HEATHER! STOP!! YOU'VE GOT ME ALL WRONG!

I DON'T WANT TO HARM YOU--EITHER OF YOU! IT WAS FOR YOU THAT I DID IT--I'VE ALWAYS LOVED YOU!

DON'T YOU HEAR ME, WOMAN? I LOVE YOU!

BUT YOUR MOTHER KEPT RIGHT ON HATING--AND THROWING ROCKS.

NOT MANY OF THEM FOUND THEIR TARGET, OF COURSE.

THIS IS YOUR LAST CHANCE, WOMAN. COME WITH ME--IF NOT FOR YOUR OWN SAKE--THEN FOR THE BOY'S!

DO YOU WANT HIM TO DIE OUT HERE, IN THE MIDDLE OF NOWHERE?

DO YOU??

AT LAST, YOUR MOTHER ANSWERED,

YES!

THAT'S WHAT I DO WANT--IF LIVING MEANS SHARING THE SAME WORLD WITH YOU!

LET MY SON GROW UP TO KILL YOU WITH HIS OWN TWO HANDS--OR LET HIM DIE, LIKE HIS FATHER!

ANY WAY YOU WANT IT, HEATHER...

STILL, I RATHER SUSPECT YOU'LL FEEL DIFFERENTLY, WHEN YOU SEE THE FIRST SIGNS OF NUMBNESS SET IN.

GOOD-BYE, HEATHER.

I-I'M GLAD YOU THREW ROCKS AT HIM, MOTHER. I'M GLAD!

DON'T TALK, DARLING. SAVE YOUR STRENGTH... FOR CLIMBING BACK UP... IF WE CAN.

ARE YOU READY, DANNY? ARE YOU READY TO TRY??

YES, MOTHER. YES, I'M...

...READY!

THAT IS **GOOD.** FOR, TO BECOME **ONE** OF US--TO EAT OF THE **TREE OF IMMORTALITY,** AND THUS TO GAIN **ETERNAL LIFE** HERE IN K'UN-LUN YOU FIRST MUST MEET--

--THE **CHALLENGE OF THE ONE!**

I HAVE FELLED **MANY** MEN WITH EASE, O YU-TI.

SHALL I FLINCH AT **ONE?**

BE **CERTAIN,** MY **SON,** THAT SUCH FALSE BRAVADO IS NOT THE VOICE OF A **DEMON** AT YOUR EAR...

FOR, ONE MAY PERHAPS **BE** MANY... AYE, AND **MORE** THAN MANY...

...WHEN THAT ONE IS **SHU-HU!**

HE WHOSE LIPS ARE PLEDGED TO **SILENCE,** AND WHOSE NAME MEANS THE **LIGHTNING...**

...AND WHOSE **FISTS** ARE LIKE TWIN **THUNDERBOLTS!**

WELL, MY **SON?** WILL YOU **FACE** SHU-HU...

OR SHALL MY **DRAGON-KINGS** AND I DELAY THIS CHALLENGE UNTIL **ANOTHER** DAY, WHEN YOU ARE **RESTED?**

NO, AUGUST ONE. MY TRIAL BY COMBAT **MUST** BE TODAY. I WILL **NOT** DELAY IT.

THEN **PROCEED.** LET IT **BE** AS IT IS **WRITTEN.**

CALMLY, **RESOLUTELY,** YOU STRIDE TO THE **CENTER** OF THE EERIE INDOOR AMPHI-THEATRE.

YOU AND THE LIGHTNING-LORD **BOW** TO EACH OTHER, FOR THAT IS THE **WAY** OF THE EAST...

...AND NOWHERE MORE SO THAN IN K'UN-LUN.

THEN--THE **BATTLE!**

SHU-HU IS **SWIFT**--NEARLY AS SWIFT AS THE **THUNDERCLAPS** FOR WHICH HE IS NAMED.

YET, YOU WHO ONCE WERE DANNY RAND **EVADE** HIS MAM-MOTH FIST, AND STRIKE HOME A SOLID **BODY BLOW...**

--TO NO EFFECT!

STARTLED, YOU SHOVE YOUR HARD, CALLOUSED **PALM** AGAINST THE MASSIVE CHIN BEFORE YOU-- PUSH IT **BACK**, WITH FORCE ENOUGH TO SNAP A MAN'S **NECK**--

WHAK!

--AND, THE NEXT INSTANT, ARE NEARLY **SHATTERED** FOR YOUR PAINS!...

ALMOST **UN-BELIEVING** NOW, YOU SEEK TO TAKE ADVANTAGE OF THE SLOW **PONDEROUSNESS** OF THE HOODED MAN'S VAST **BULK**.

THDD

HAI-YA!

YOUR NIMBLE **FEET** FIND THEIR TARGET, SURELY ENOUGH--

BUT, ONCE MORE, SHU-HU SEEMS SCARCELY **SHAKEN** BY THE IMPACT--

WOM

--HIS **OWN** CLENCHED FISTS ARE **FAR** FROM SLOW--

--AND ONLY A **NEAR-DECADE** OF INTENSIVE TRAINING ENABLES YOU TO **REGAIN** YOUR FOOTING--

THUP

PHIK THIK THIK THIK

SO, AUGUST ONE... THIS **GAUDILY-FESTOONED** WEAKLING IS HE WHOM YOU WOULD WELCOME INTO THE COMPANY OF THE **IMMORTALS!?**

--INSTEAD OF BEING **SMASHED** AGAINST THE WALL, LIKE A WORRISOME **BUG**.

RATHER, IT SEEMS TO *THIS* ONE THAT HE SHOULD BE TURNED OUT AGAIN INTO THE *END-LESS* SNOWS THAT DRIFT BE-YOND THE *GATE OF DREAMS.*

THE AUGUST PERSONAGE OF JADE SAYS *NOTHING.*

AND, IF THE BROW BEHIND HIS SOMBRE HOOD IS *FURROWED,* NOT EVEN THE *FOUR DRAGON-KINGS* STAND CLOSE ENOUGH TO *SEE.*

MEANWHILE, WITH SURPRISING *QUICKNESS,* THE GIANT HURLS HIM-SELF *BODILY* TOWARD YOU.

WITH AN AGILE LEAP, YOU *DODGE* FEET WHOSE SHEER MASS COULD CRUSH A *TIGER'S* SKULL...

...ONLY TO BE FELLED IN TURN BY A FAST-DARTING FIST.

BLDT

AGAIN, AND YET *AGAIN,* THOSE MASSIVE HANDS *PUMMEL* YOU...

...*TEACH* YOU WHAT THE *AFTERLIFE* MUST BE LIKE, BEYOND *K'U-CH'U-CH'IAO,* THE BRIDGE OF PAIN, BENEATH WHICH FLOW RIVERS OF *CRIMSON.*

FWYM

IN DESPERATION, YOU ALLOW YOURSELF TO BE STRUCK ONCE MORE AGAINST A *FAR WALL*--

THAP!

--FROM WHICH YOU *RICOCHET,* IN TURN--

PKOW

--IN AN ATTEMPT TO GAIN A MOMENT'S *RESPITE.*

DWOP!

AN ATTEMPT WHICH PROVES MOST *VAIN!*

IT SEEMS TO BE *SLIPPING AWAY* NOW--YOUR GRIP ON *CONSCIOUSNESS.*

BUT *WHY*, THEN, DOES YOUR MIND RACE BACK ONCE MORE TO THAT WINDBLOWN LEDGE?

WHY DO YOU HEAR AGAIN YOUR *MOTHER'S* VOICE, FROM OUT OF THE *DEAD PAST?*

WOULD IT NOT BE *SIMPLER* FAR TO *LET IT GO*-- TO COLLAPSE INTO SWEET *OBLIVION?*

COME ON, *DANNY!* WE'RE GOING TO *CLIMB* NOW...!

YOUR HEART BEATS *FASTER* WITHIN YOUR *BREAST...*

BUT, IS IT *HERE* THAT IT BEATS... HERE, WITHIN THE ARENA OF YOUR THROBBING *PAIN...*

...OR IS IT *THERE*, WHERE TWO PEOPLE MADE THAT MOST *INHUMAN* EFFORT, TEN YEARS GONE?

YOU MADE IT *THEN*, DIDN'T YOU?

SOMEHOW, IT WAS *EASIER* THEN, IN SPITE OF THE NUMBING *COLD...* IN SPITE OF THE VIVID MEMORY OF *MURDER MOST FOUL!*

FOR, THOUGH YOU KNEW YOU BOTH WERE *LOST...*

...THAT YOU WERE HEADING *FORWARD*, INTO THE *UNKNOWN*, INSTEAD OF BACK TOWARD *MEACHUM* AND THE *DEATH* THAT WAITED SURELY AT HIS HANDS...

...STILL, YOU HAD *EACH OTHER.*

PROMISE ME YOU DON'T HATE YOUR *FATHER* FOR BRINGING YOU HERE!

DANNY, I... I WANT YOU TO *PROMISE* ME SOME- THING.

FOR, HE HAD A VISION OF A *BETTER WORLD*, WAITING SOME- WHERE FOR THE *THREE* OF US...

...SOMEWHERE ALWAYS JUST BEYOND THE NEXT *RIDGE.*

PROMISE ME, DANNY!

I...*PROMISE*, MOTHER.

AND SO YOU *WANDERED* ALONE, FOR DAYS. THEN, EVEN AS YOUR STRENGTH GREW EVER *WEAKER...*

..YOUR STEPS EVER MORE *FALTERING...*

...SUDDENLY, YOU BOTH WEREN'T *ALONE* ANY LONGER.

THE WOLVES MUST HAVE TRAILED YOU BOTH FOR HOURS, IN PATIENT, SINISTER SILENCE.

BUT NOW, THEY BEGAN TO RUN... AS IF SENSING SOMEHOW THAT THEY HAD LITTLE TIME LEFT...

MOTHER...WHAT KIND OF PLACE WAS FATHER LOOKING FOR? I... I NEVER KNEW...

IT WAS A DREAM PLACE, DANNY. IT NEVER REALLY EXISTED, EXCEPT IN HIS OWN MIND...

...ALTHOUGH ONCE... JUST FOR A LITTLE WHILE...I THOUGHT THAT PERHAPS IT DID.

IT WAS THE VERY NEXT SECOND THAT SHE SAW IT...

NO! IT-- IT CAN'T BE--!

A BRIDGE! OUT HERE IN THE MIDDLE OF NOWHERE!

COULD IT BE THE ONE THAT LEADS TO--NO! THAT'S IMPOSSIBLE!

THAT PLACE DOESN'T EXIST! IT COULDN'T!

IT WAS THEN, YOU REMEMBER, THAT THE HOWLING BEGAN...

IT'S...JUST A BRIDGE... NOTHING MORE.

...THE HOWLING THAT WAS SCARCELY MORE HORRIFYING THAN THE SUDDEN, TERRIBLE KNOWLEDGE THAT THEY HAD BEEN THERE, ALL ALONG.

ARROOO

WOLVES!

RUN, DANNY! RUN FOR THE BRIDGE!

HURRY, DARLING! HURRY!

THE BRIDGE LEADS OUT--OVER A **CHASM.**

MAYBE THEY WON'T **FOLLOW** US ACROSS IT. MAYBE--

BUT, YOU ALSO KNEW THAT IN AN INSTANT THEY'D BE **AFTER** YOU AGAIN...THAT THEY'D BE UPON YOU BEFORE YOU REACHED THE **OTHER** SIDE...

YOU BOTH LOOKED BACK...SAW THE SNOW-WOLVES **PAUSE** FOR A MOMENT...

...UNLESS...!

THE **FEAR** WAS WELLING UP WITHIN YOU THEN. THE FEAR FOR YOUR OWN BRIEF **LIFE.**

YOU DIDN'T EVEN **SEE** HER, AS SHE TURNED--RACED BACK TOWARD THE RAVENING WOLVES...

SO YOU NEVER **NOTICED** WHEN THE SOUND OF YOUR OWN FEET, SLAPPING AGAINST THE CREAKING BOARDS...

...BECAME THE **ONLY** SOUND THAT ROSE ABOVE THE BAYING OF WOLVES AND WIND.

--AND *HURLED HERSELF INTO THEIR MIDST!*

YOU ONLY HEARD THE HOWLING TURN TO **SNARLS**...

...AND **ONCE,** PERHAPS, ABOVE THE WIND... A WOMAN'S INVOLUNTARY **SCREAM!**

YOU **PAUSED** THEN--NOT QUITE ON THE OTHER SIDE OF THE BRIDGE. YOU **TURNED,** CONFUSED...

MOTHER...?

MOTHER!!

MOTHER--!

YOU SAW THEN-- WHAT YOU *SAW.* AND YOU'LL NEVER *FORGET* IT. YET, AS YOU STARTED *BACK* TO HER, HEEDLESS OF THE COST, MINDLESS OF THE FANGED *PERIL*--

--SUDDENLY, STRONG HANDS WERE THERE--GRIPPING, HOLDING--

AND, THE *NEXT INSTANT*--

THWISSSH!

YOU DIDN'T *WONDER* THEN AT THE *MEN* WHO HAD APPEARED AS IF FROM NOWHERE--AT THE WEAPON OF *ANOTHER AGE* WHICH HAD FIRED--*TOO LATE!*

SHE...IS *DEAD.*

MOTHER--!? I--I'VE GOT TO--

BUT *YOU* ARE AMONG THE *LIVING* ONCE MORE.

WELCOME, LAD...

...WELCOME TO *K'UN-LUN!*

...WITH *TOO MANY KINDS* OF *PAIN*...PAIN OF A *DIFFERENT* KIND FROM THAT YOU FEEL *TODAY,* THOUGH NO LESS *REAL* FOR ALL THAT.

BUT NOW, THE *REALITIES* COME POURING OVER YOU AGAIN, LIKE A *TIDAL WAVE* OF AGONY...

...LIKE A *THUNDERCLOUD* OF *DARK DESPAIR*...

YOU DIDN'T EVEN *HEAR* HIM THEN, DID YOU? YOUR *TEARS* WERE TOO LOUD, YOUR *SORROW* TOO STRIDENT... YOUR YOUNG BODY TOO WRACKED...

...LIKE THE SHADOW OF *DEATH* ITSELF!

I AM *IRON FIST!* I WAS TRAINED TO BE A *LIVING WEAPON*-- TO DEFEND MYSELF FROM *ANYTHING HUMAN!*

YET YOU TOSS ME ABOUT-- LIKE A *CHILD'S BROKEN PLAYTHING!*

WHO ARE YOU??

YOUR ONLY ANSWER:

A BLUR OF DEADLY MOTION, STREAKING FROM OUT OF YOUR TORMENTOR'S VERY HAND--

ZZIP!

--TO TAKE SOLID FORM IN YOUR OWN PAIN-WRACKED SHOULDER!

THEN, EVEN AS YOU REALIZE AT LAST THAT YOUR OPPONENT IS NOT HUMAN--

THUK!

--SOMEONE ELSE IS MYSTERIOUSLY THERE!

PERHAPS IT IS THE SIGHT OF HER--MORE REAL EVEN THAN THE DUST AND CARNAGE OF THE ARENA--WHICH BRINGS YOU INSTANTLY TO YOUR SENSES--

TLUNK!

--SO THAT THE SECOND SWIFT-HURLED BLADE DOES NOT FIND ITS MARK!

IT IS FOR HER YOU HAVE BEEN FIGHTING, ALL ALONG!

SHE DIED TO BRING YOU TO THIS PLACE CALLED K'UN-LUN--A PLACE IN WHICH SHE DID NOT EVEN BELIEVE, AND WHICH SHE THUS COULD NEVER HOPE TO ENTER.

YOU HEAR HER VOICE ONCE AGAIN, FROM OUT OF THE PAST--AND IT DULLS THE PAIN YOU FEEL--

--DULLS IT INTO INSENSITIVITY, THEN OBLIVION.

NO LONGER DO YOU FEEL THE PAIN--

--AND THE BLOOD WHICH DROPS COULD AS EASILY BELONG TO A CHILD WHO PERISHED TEN YEARS AGO.

NOW, YOU ARE MERELY-- IRON FIST!

AND, YOU ARE AS WELL-- A MAN GONE BERSERK!

HAI--

--YAH!

DRAK!

YOU KNOW YOU FAILED BEFORE-- WITH BLOWS YOU THOUGHT YOUR STRONGEST.

BUT THAT DOESN'T MATTER NOW, AS YOU LEAP ANEW INTO THE JAWS OF STEEL-FLESHED DOOM--

--AS YOU STRIKE AGAIN--

WHUMP!

--AND AGAIN--

BKKK

--AND YET AGAIN--

NOW, YOU CAN FEEL THE HARD, MAN-FORGED METAL BENEATH THE HOOD--FEEL IT START TO GIVE AND BEND AND TWIST.

THE PONDEROUS GIANT'S MOVES BECOME SLUGGISH-- SLOW--MECHANICAL--

AND, IF HE--IF IT COULD FEEL PAIN--

FWHAKK!

--ITS PAIN WOULD DWARF ANY THAT YOU HAVE EVER KNOWN!

AT LAST IT TOTTERS-- REELS--YET, IT IS STILL TOO STRONG TO FALL.

AND NOW, AN ICY CALM SETTLES OVER YOU--

--A CALM WHICH IS, FINALLY, YOUR GREATEST STRENGTH.

YOU CALL SILENTLY, INWARDLY, UPON THE INVINCIBLE WILL WHICH FORMS THE VERY CORE OF YOUR BEING.

UNFATHOMED RESERVES OF CONCENTRATION AND RE- SOLVE FLOW FROM YOUR BRAIN, YOUR SHOULDERS, YOUR LEGS, FROM EVERY PART OF A BODY HONED FOR TEN LONG YEARS--

...IELD, MERGE, AND... CE--

--INTO YOUR HAND--

--UNTIL IT BECOMES LIKE UNTO--

--A THING OF IRON!

YOU DO NOT EVEN NEED TO *LOOK* AT IT, DO YOU? YOU *KNOW* THE STRENGTH THAT IS THERE.

YOU CAN SENSE THE *SHEER, NAKED POWER* WHICH RADIATES FROM YOUR CLENCHED HAND, AS IF WITH A *LIFE* ALL ITS OWN.

NOW, MORE THAN *EVER*--

NOW, PERHAPS REALLY FOR THE *FIRST* TIME--

-- YOU ARE *IRON FIST*--

SHK-O!

--AND YOU ARE *TRIUMPHANT!*

WHRRRR

KLUMP!

I CAN SEE IT *CLEARLY* NOW, O AUGUST PERSONAGE... AND YOU *DRAGON-KINGS...*

FIRST, THE CHALLENGE OF THE *MANY*... THEN OF THE *ONE*...

AND LASTLY, THE CHALLENGE OF *MYSELF*-- OF MY *WILL* TO LIVE --OF MY *FITNESS* TO LIVE!

I STAND BLOODY-- BUT UN- BOWED. NEVER BOWED!

AND I CLAIM, AT LAST--THE *RIGHT* WHICH NOW IS *MINE* TO CLAIM!

THEN, SLOWLY, IN DEEP SEPULCHRAL TONES, COMES THE ANSWER YOU *KNEW* WOULD COME.

YES, MY SON. YOU HAVE *WON*-- THE RIGHT IS YOURS!

THE RIGHT TO CHOOSE BETWEEN *IMMORTALITY*-- ETERNAL LIFE --

--AND *DEATH!*

End of Chapter 1.

Chapter 2:
HEART OF THE DRAGON!

YOU ARE *IRON FIST*-- AND THE ODORS THAT ASSAULT YOUR TENDER NOSTRILS THIS NIGHT FILL YOU WITH A GROWING FEELING OF REVULSION.

YOU HAVE HEARD MANY STORIES OF THIS STRANGE PLACE CALLED NEW YORK-- THIS CITY THAT IS HARDLY MORE THAN A MEMORY TO YOU--

--AND, UNFORTUNATELY, IT SEEMS THAT ALL THE TALES ARE *TRUE*.

DAILY RATES

STILL, YOU DRAW UPON YOUR INNER RESOURCES-- *CLOSE* YOUR WELL-HONED SENSES TO THE *OFFEN-SIVENESS* THAT SURROUNDS YOU--AS YOU *CONCENTRATE* ONCE MORE UPON YOUR *MISSION*--

--FOR YOU HAVE COME TO THIS MUCH-BEGRIMED METROPOLIS TO *KILL* A MAN--AND YOU CANNOT *REST* UNTIL THE DEED IS *DONE*!

IN YOUR MIND'S EYE, YOU SEE HIS *FACE*--AND FURY GROWS WITHIN YOU AT THE *SIGHT* OF IT--

--BUT IT IS FURY CAST QUICKLY *ASIDE*--AS A SOUND INTERRUPTS YOUR GRIM REVERIE.

THE SOUND IS A *MOAN*--AND IT DRIFTS DESPERATELY FROM THE SHADOWS OF THIS ALLEYWAY.

SILENTLY, ALMOST CAT-LIKE, YOU STRIDE INTO THE DARKNESS, PURSUING THE ELUSIVE *WHISPER.*

A *DEAD-END* LOOMS BEFORE YOU--THE HACKLES RISE ABRUPTLY ON YOUR *NECK*--

--AND YOU CURSE YOURSELF FOR A *FOOL* TO HAVE WALKED SO WILLINGLY INTO A *TRAP!*

LOOKIN' FOR SOMETHING, PAL?

YOU HAVE SEEN THEIR TYPE *BEFORE*--THE LOW, SLOPING *BROWS*--THE CRUEL *TIGHTNESS* AT THE CORNERS OF THEIR EYES...

THEY ARE CONFIDENT--PERHAPS *TOO* CONFIDENT--AND THUS THEY ARE VULNERABLE!

STEP ASIDE AND LET ME *PASS*, PLEASE! YOU HAVE NO BUSINESS WITH *ME!*

WRONG, FRIEND--WE GOT *TEN G's* WORTH'A BUSINESS WITH YOU.

--*DEAD* OR ALIVE, IT SAYS --

SOME BIGSHOT PUT OUT A *CONTRACT* ON ANY DUDE WEARING THIS *DRAGON BRAND*--

--AN', BUDDY, WE AIM TO *COLLECT* THAT DOUGH-- ANY WAY WE *HAVE* TO!

THEY COME AT YOU *WILDLY*, WEAPONS FLASHING IN THE DIM LIGHT --

YOU CALM YOURSELF INWARDLY...

--THEN MEET SLASHING *PIPE* AND *KNIFE-BLADE* WITH THE SKILLS FEW MEN SAVE *YOU* HAVE MASTERED.

FKXK!

HOK

WEAPONLESS, YOUR ASSAILANTS ARE HARDLY A *MATCH*--

--FOR A WELL-PLACED *ELEPHANT KICK*--

--OR THE *BLOW* OF THE *HAMMER.*

WHUDD!

PWOM

YOUR TWO ATTACKERS SPRAWL TO THE *GROUND*--AND ARE INSTANTLY REPLACED BY THEIR *COM-PANIONS*--

--BUT A *LOCKING BLOCK* TURNS ASIDE THE BAYONET STROKE OF ONE ...

--WHILE A *BEAR THRUST* STEALS AWAY THE *BREATH* OF THE OTHER.

CHUK!

THE *SWORD HAND* CONVINCES THE FINAL AGGRESSOR TO TOSS HIS *BLADE* ASIDE --

--AND PERHAPS HIS IN-VOLUNTARY *SCREAM* IS WHAT PREVENTS YOU FROM HEARING THE *FOOTSTEPS* BEHIND YOU --

SPLANG!

--UNTIL IT IS FAR *TOO LATE!*

YOU STUMBLE TO YOUR *KNEES*, YOUR HEAD *REELING* FROM THE *PAIN*--

--AND THE MEMORIES COME FLOODING BACK UNBIDDEN.

AGAIN, YOU ARE THE *BOY* YOU WERE TEN YEARS AGO. AGAIN, YOU ARE *AFRAID*--

--AND AGAIN, YOUR INNOCENT'S EYES GROW WIDE AS YOU FIRST BEHOLD THE MOUNTAIN CALLED *K'UN LUN.*

AGAIN, YOU REMEMBER THE *AWE* YOU FELT AS YOU PASSED FOR THE FIRST TIME THRU THE ANCIENT CITY'S *GATES*--

--THE FEELING THAT YOU WERE ENTERING NOT A CITY, BUT A *FANTASY*-- AND THAT TO *DISBELIEVE* IN THE DREAM WOULD SURELY BE *SACRILEGE.*

AND AGAIN, YOUR HEART BEATS *MADLY* IN YOUR CHEST--AS YOU ARE USHERED INTO THE PRESENCE OF THE VENERABLE *YU-TI*, HE WHO IS CALLED THE *AUGUST PERSONAGE OF JADE*...

MAY YOUR STAY WITH US BE A *REWARDING* ONE.

WELCOME, DANIEL RAND--TO THE CITY OF *K'UN LUN.*

WE KNOW OF YOUR FATHER'S *FATE*, MY SON--AND THE FATE OF YOUR *MOTHER* AS WELL-- AND OUR HEARTS *GRIEVE* OPENLY FOR THEM!

TO LOSE ONE'S *PARENTS* IS TO LOSE THE ROOTS OF *HERITAGE.*

STILL, WE SHALL TRY TO MAKE YOU *HAPPY* HERE, DANIEL!

IF THERE IS EVER ANYTHING YOU *WANT*, MERELY NAME IT--

--AND IT WILL BE *YOURS!*

THERE'S ONLY *ONE* THING *I* WANT, MISTER...

I WANT REVENGE!!

TROUBLED, ILL AT EASE, YOU WENT TO THE CHAMBERS OF YÜ-TI...

HOODED ONE, THESE PAST YEARS, LEI KUNG HAS TAUGHT ME SKILLS I WOULD NOT HAVE DREAMED *POSSIBLE*..

--AND 'THOUGH I AM TOLD I HAVE *MASTERED* THEM...

BUT YOU *HAVE* MASTERED THEM, MY SON. OF ALL WHO HAVE EVER BEEN STUDENTS OF *THE WAY*, YOU ARE BY FAR THE *BEST*--

--AND YET I SENSE YOUR SOUL RESTS *UNEASY.* TELL ME, DANIEL -- *WHY?*

AUGUST ONE, PLEASE-- DO NOT THINK ME *UNGRATEFUL* FOR ALL YOU HAVE GIVEN ME--

--BUT IT IS *NOT ENOUGH!*

MEMORIES: FOR LESS THAN AN *INSTANT* YOUR MIND HAS WANDERED *THRU* THEM--

--BUT FOR ONE IN YOUR *UN-ENVIABLE* POSITION, EVEN SO *BRIEF* A DISTRACTION CAN PROVE QUITE *FATAL.*

THE ONE WHO STANDS BEHIND YOU *CLENCHES* HIS JAW-MUSCLES AS HE PREPARES TO DELIVER THE *DEATH-BLOW*--

--BUT THAT SPLIT-SECOND OF *HESITATION* IS AMPLE TIME FOR YOU TO REACT!

SPAK!

YOU WHIRL--A LIGHTNING KICK JARRING THE HEAVY *BLUDGEON* FROM HIS HAND--

--AND YOUR FOLLOW-THROUGH BRINGS YOU *FACE-TO-FACE* WITH YOUR ATTACKERS.

THEY'VE ALL REGAINED THEIR *FOOTING* AND STAND POISED TO RENEW THE ASSAULT--

--BUT YOUR SUDDEN *RECOVERY* HAS STARTLED THEM--

CHUD!

--AND THAT IS AN ADVANTAGE YOU QUICKLY PUT TO THE *BEST* OF USE!

PWOK!

YOUR ASSAILANTS ARE **NOT** INTELLIGENT MEN--BUT EVEN THEY QUICKLY REALIZE THAT NO REWARD IS WORTH SUCH SKILLFULLY-INFLICTED PAIN.

THEY **FLEE**--

OKAY, FREAK, SCORE ONE FER YOU--BUT YOU AIN'T HEARD THE **LAST** OF THIS!

AND YOU STAND, BATHED IN THE SWEAT OF YOUR **EXERTION**, WONDERING WHO COULD HAVE KNOWN OF YOUR **COMING**--

--AND PLACED SUCH A PRICE ON YOUR HEAD.

THEN, FINDING NO ANSWERS, YOU SURVEY YOUR INJURIES... BONES INTACT--BRUISES **SUPERFICIAL**--

--AND, ALMOST ACCIDENTALLY, YOUR FINGERS BRUSH THE DRAGON BRANDED ON YOUR CHEST-- THE DRAGON THAT **MARKED** YOU TO THESE MEN.

YOU **CONSIDER** THE DRAGON--THEN NOTICE YOUR WEAPON-HANDS--

...AND AGAIN THE MEMORIES COME...

YOUR HANDS: YOU WORKED DILIGENTLY TO **CONDITION** THEM AS LEI KUNG SAID YOU MUST--

--THRUSTING THEM CEASELESSLY INTO A DEEP TUB OF **SAND**--TO BUILD THE CALLUS AND DEADEN THE PAIN--

--AND, WHEN THE SAND WAS NO LONGER ENOUGH, INTO **GRAVEL**--

--AND, AT LAST, INTO BUCKETS OF **ROCK**--

--UNTIL YOUR HANDS BECAME AS THE ROCK--UNFEELING, **IRRESISTIBLE**--

HAI!

THRACK!

THE GREAT HORNED HEAD LUNGED FORWARD, UNBEARABLE *BREATH* SEARING THE FLESH OF YOUR *CHEEK*--

--AS YOU *LEAPT* TO ONE SIDE, DELIVERING A *DEVASTATING ROCK-SMASH BLOW*--

THUD!

--WHICH *STUNNED* THE UNDYING ONE AS INTENDED--

--BUT FOR ONLY AN *INSTANT*--

--AFTER WHICH YOU FOUND YOURSELF FACED WITH THE SAME NIGH-IMPOSSIBLE *PROBLEM:*

HOW DO I *DEFEAT* A CREATURE WHO CANNOT BE *KILLED?*

FOR A MOMENT, YOU *PONDERED* THIS--

--THEN, A SILENT *PRAYER* UPON YOUR LIPS--

--YOU HURLED YOURSELF BOLDLY AT THE STRANGELY-SHAPED *SCAR* UPON THE DRAGON-LORD'S *BREAST*--

--FOR IT WAS *THRU* THIS SCAR THAT SHOU-LAO'S *HEART* WAS TAKEN--

--THRU THIS SCAR THAT THE UNDYING ONE RECEIVED THE MYSTIC *EMANATIONS* THAT ETERNALLY *SUSTAINED* HIM--

--AND IF THOSE EMANATIONS WERE TO BE SOMEHOW *BLOCKED OFF*--

--BY A *BODY*, PERHAPS?--

--BY *YOUR BODY*--

--THEN WHO COULD SAY WHAT MIGHT *OCCUR?*

THE *HEAT* POURING FROM THE SCAR WAS ALMOST *UNIMAGINABLE* AND THOUGH YOU COULD FEEL THE FLESH *BLISTERING* ON YOUR CHEST...

--STILL YOU *MAINTAINED* YOUR HOLD--

--UNTIL *UNCONSCIOUSNESS* HAD CREEPED ALMOST *UPON YOU*--

--AND THEN--*ABRUPTLY*--YOUR PERSEVERANCE WAS *REWARDED*--

--BUT YOUR EFFORTS HAD INDELIBLY *MARKED* YOU TILL THE END OF YOUR DAYS.

STILL, YOU HAD *TRIUMPHED*--AND THUS HAD EARNED THE RIGHT TO *CLAIM* YOUR PRIZE!

THE CAVERN WAS NOT *DEEP*--AND THE STENCH OF *DECAY* THAT POURED FROM IT SWEPT ACROSS YOU LIKE A *WAVE!*

DETERMINEDLY, YOU *SHOOK* YOUR HEAD--TOOK ONE LONG LAST CLEAN *BREATH*--THEN STRODE INTO THE *DARKNESS*--

RESPECTFULLY, YOU *APPROACHED* THE SEETHING MASS--*BOWED* TO IT GENTLY--THEN RAISED YOUR HANDS IN *SALUTE*--

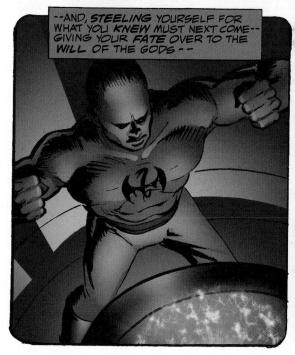

--AND, *STEELING* YOURSELF FOR WHAT YOU *KNEW* MUST NEXT COME-- GIVING YOUR *FATE* OVER TO THE *WILL* OF THE GODS --

--AND FOUND IT A DARKNESS *BROKEN* BY THE LIGHT FROM A HIDEOUSLY-CARVED *BRAZIER* STANDING IN THE CAVERN'S CENTER--A BRAZIER THAT BUBBLED AND PULSED AS IF IT HAD A LIFE OF ITS OWN--

--AND, IN TRUTH, IT *DID*--

--FOR YOU BEHELD AT LAST, THE LIVING, BEATING SOUL OF *SHOU-LAO, THE UNDYING* --

THIS WAS THE *HEART OF THE DRAGON!*

-- YOU PLUNGED YOUR OPEN HANDS AGONIZINGLY INTO THE GLOWING MOLTEN *ESSENCE* --

--AND WHEN FINALLY YOU *PULLED* THEM FROM THE DRAGON'S HEART--

--THEY *FAIRLY* SEEMED TO *SHINE!*

BUT, AT THAT MOMENT, FINDING THE *EXTENT* OF YOUR *NEWLY-GAINED* POWERS WAS *SECONDARY* TO FINDING *RELIEF* FOR YOUR SMOLDERING HANDS.

EAGERLY, YOU STAGGERED OUT INTO THE WELCOMING *SNOW* AND...

THANKS, JOKER--FOR SAVING ME THE BOTHER OF *HUNT-ING* YOU DOWN!

THOSE OTHER *PUNKS* *TOLD* ME YOU WERE IN THE *NEIGH-BORHOOD*-- TOLD ME WHAT YOU *DID* TO THEM--

--BUT YOU WON'T HAVE A *CHANCE* TO TRY YOUR TRICKS ON-- *SCYTHE!*

I DO NOT WISH ANY *TROUBLE!*

MAYBE *NOT*--BUT YOU'VE *GOT IT!*

YOU'RE WORTH *TEN THOUSAND DOLLARS* TO THE MAN WHO BRINGS YOU IN!

--AND FOR *THAT* KIND OF MONEY, I DON'T PLAY *GAMES!*

--AND, AS DARKNESS THREATENS TO PULL YOU DOWN FOREVER, THE MEMORIES COME ONCE AGAIN...

ONE WEEK PAST: IT IS YOUR DAY OF *DESTINY.* YOU STAND IN THE PRESENCE OF *YÜ-TI* AND THE *LUNG-WANG*-- THE FOUR *DRAGON-KINGS*--AS THE AUGUST ONE ADDRESSES YOU--

ARE YOU *READY,* MY SON, TO BE *CHALLENGED*--

--TO PROVE YOUR-SELF *WORTHY* OF JOINING THE COMPANY OF *IMMORTALS?*

I HUMBLY AWAIT YOUR *PLEASURE,* O *FATHER-HEAVEN.*

THUS YOU MET THE *CHALLENGE* OF THE MANY-- FOUR MARTIAL-ARTS MASTERS WHO FELL LIKE *BRITTLE CHINA DOLLS* BEFORE YOU--

KTHOK

TTAP!

--THEN THE *CHALLENGE* OF THE ONE --THE CHALLENGE OF *SHU-HU,* CALLED THE *LIGHTNING*--

SHKOW!

--REVEALED AT LAST TO BE A *ROBOT*-- BY YOUR AWESOME *IRON FIST*--

--AND FINALLY...

MY SON, YOU HAVE *WON* THE RIGHT TO CHOOSE BETWEEN *ETERNAL LIFE* --AND *DEATH!*

I AM *READY,* HOODED ONE!

THEN *COME* WITH ME, DANIEL --TO THE *TREE OF IMMORTALITY!*

SHORTLY, IN THE ANCIENT CITY'S SPRAWL-ING *PLAZA...*

YOU KNOW THE LEGEND OF OUR CITY, DANIEL--HOW THE *K'UN LUN MOUNTAIN* APPEARS IN THE WORLD OF MEN FOR ONLY *ONE* DAY OUT OF EVERY *TEN* YEARS!

ON SUCH A DAY YOU FIRST *CAME* TO US --AND ON SUCH A DAY YOU MAY *LEAVE* -- IF SUCH IS YOUR *WISH*--

THEN MY *CHOICE* IS GREATER THAN I *SUPPOSED,* O YÜ-TI!

--FOR *TOMORROW* IS THAT MOST SACRED DAY IN A *DECADE*!

TO *EAT* OF THE FRUIT OF THE *TREE OF IMMORTALITY* AND DWELL AMONG THE *ETERNAL PEOPLE* OF *K'UN LUN FOREVER*--

--OR TO PASS TO-MORROW *OUT* THRU THE CITY'S GATES AND INTO THE WORLD OF MEN--NEVER TO *RETURN* HERE!

THEN *MAKE YOUR DECISION,* MY SON--AND *EAT* OF THE FRUIT I'VE PLUCKED FOR YOU.

I WANT TO, AUGUST ONE-- *BELIEVE* ME WHEN I SAY THAT-- BUT I *CANNOT*!

TOMORROW I AM GOING BACK TO *CIVILIZATION*-- TO FIND *HAROLD MEACHUM,* THE MAN WHO *MURDERED* MY FATHER!

THEN ALL THE YEARS YOU HAVE SPENT AMONG US HAVE NOT *DIMMED* THE FIRES OF *REVENGE* IN YOUR HEART, DANIEL!

NO, YÜ-TI--THEY HAVE *NOT*!

I'VE *TRIED* TO QUENCH THEM-- TRIED TO *BLOT THEM OUT*-- BUT EVERY NIGHT, THE IMAGE OF MY FATHER HURTLING TO HIS *DOOM* AWAKENS ME IN A SWEAT.

BUT WHAT WILL REVENGE GAIN YOU? WILL IT PRO-VIDE *SUCCOR* FOR YOUR SOUL?

I WILL NOT-- *CANNOT*--REST UNTIL MEACHUM HAS *PAID* FOR HIS CRIME!

HATRED IS A FLOWER WHOSE ROOTS *STRANGLE* ALL THEY ENCOMPASS, MY SON!

HATRED? WHAT COULD *YOU* KNOW OF HATRED, OLD MAN? WHAT COULD AN *IMMORTAL* KNOW OF THE *PAIN* OF A LOVED ONE'S DEATH?

I KNOW *MORE* THAN YOU COULD IMAGINE, DANIEL--

--FOR WENDELL RAND WAS NOT ONLY YOUR *FATHER*--

--HE WAS ALSO MY *BROTHER*!

YÜ-TI'S ANSWER *STUNS* YOU--

--BUT IT DOES NOT PREVENT YOUR *LEAVING* K'UN LUN MOUNTAIN THE NEXT MORN-ING AS *INTENDED*.

AND, AS THE *GATES* OF THE MYSTICAL CITY FADED IN THE MISTS BEHIND YOU, PERHAPS YOU FELT A TINGE OF *REGRET*...

--FOR THIS TIME ADAM WAS NOT CAST OUT OF PARADISE...

...THIS TIME HE STALKED OUT OF HIS OWN ACCORD...

--AND YOU FIGHT OFF THE ENCROACHING BLACKNESS TO SEE RAZORED DEATH WHISTLING TOWARDS YOUR THROAT!

--STEEL-CABLE MUSCLES HALT THE DESCENDING BLADE--

YOU THRUST OUT A HAND--

--AND YOU CONCENTRATE-- DRAWING THE BLOOD TO YOUR BRAIN--FORCING YOURSELF BACK TO TOTAL AWARENESS!

SMOOTH *MOVE*, JOKER-- DIDN'T THINK YOU HAD *THAT* ONE STILL IN YOU!

THEN THE MAN CALLED SCYTHE TIGHTENS HIS *GRIP* ON THE CHAIN-- AND THIS TIME YOU *ALLOW* YOURSELF TO BE PULLED *OFF-BALANCE*.

FOR AN INSTANT, THE *TENSION* ON THE CHAIN GROWS SLACK--

THRUNCH!

--AND, IN THAT INSTANT--YOU *ACT*!

BUT YOUR LEATHER-GARBED OPPONENT DOES NOT LET GO OF THE CHAIN!

MAN, YOU'RE JUST *FULL* OF SURPRISES, AREN'T YOU, JOKER?

WELL, I'LL JUST HAVE TO MAKE SURE YOU DON'T PULL *THAT* ONE AGAIN!

YOU ANTICIPATE SCYTHE'S MOVE, YOUR ROCK-HARD FINGERS STRIVING DESPERATELY TO PRY THE FORGED STEEL GARROTE FROM YOUR NECK--

--BUT YOUR EFFORTS SEEM ONLY TO PULL IT THAT MUCH *TIGHTER*!

AN INVOLUNTARY *GURGLE* ESCAPES YOUR CONSTRICTED THROAT--AND SCYTHE GRINS AS HE WHIPS YOU INTO THE *SPLINTERED FENCE*--

I LET YOU GET THOSE *HANDS* ON ME-- AND I'VE HAD IT!

--BUT THAT'S A LITTLE PROBLEM I CAN EASILY *SOLVE*!

THUMP!

--AND BECOMES LIKE A THING OF IRON!

BHOM!

N-NO-- IT'S NOT POS-SIBLE!!

MY BLADE-- THE JOKER VAPORIZED IT--!

MY NAME IS NOT "JOKER", SCYTHE.

IT IS... IRON FIST!

AND I HAVE *QUESTIONS* THAT REQUIRE SWIFT ANSWERS.

NO--*NO*-- KEEP AWAY FROM ME!

YOU WERE GOING TO *KILL* ME, SCYTHE--BECAUSE A MAN PUT A *GENEROUS* PRICE ON MY HEAD.

I WANT TO KNOW *WHO*-- AND *WHY!*

OKAY--I'LL TELL YOU *ANYTHING!* ONLY DON'T PUT THOSE *HANDS* ON ME!

WH-WHY THE GUY IS AFTER YOU I DON'T *KNOW*--JUST THAT HIS NAME IS MEACHUM--

--AND THAT HE OWNS THAT UGLY *SKYSCRAPER* A FEW BLOCKS OVER!

THAT ONE?

YEAH--THAT'S IT--AND THAT'S ALL I KNOW-- *I SWEAR IT!*

NOW, PLEASE-- GO AWAY--AND LET ME *DIE* IN PEACE!

THE THING YOU LEAVE BEHIND YOU IN THE ALLEYWAY IS NO LONGER A MAN, ONLY A BROKEN, SOULLESS *HUSK.*

YOU TURN AWAY, STRIDING TOWARDS THE IMPOSING *STRUCTURE* THAT LOOMS BEFORE YOU--TOWARDS YOUR CONFRONTATION WITH THE MAN WHO KILLED YOUR FATHER!

HOW WILL HAROLD MEACHUM REACT, YOU WONDER, WHEN AT LAST, YOU STAND BEFORE HIS BROKEN, DYING FORM-- AND TELL HIM THAT *HE* IS RESPONSIBLE FOR MAKING YOU A LIVING *WEAPON?*

WILL HE SCREAM? WILL HE CRY? AT THAT POINT, WILL HE EVEN *CARE?*

End.

The Seven
Capital Cities
of Heaven

CHARACTER SKETCHES BY DAVID AJA

狗

DOG BROTHER #1

龜

FAT COBRA

虎

TIGER
BEAVTIFVL
DOVGHTER

死亡只是开始

蜘
蛛

BRIDE OF NINE SPIDERS

猴

PRINCE OF ORPHANS